Ellen R. Whitmore

She Knows How

Eleanor Early

with drawings by Jane Miller

Circle Books

The Blakiston Company—Philadelphia

"The world has but one song to sing,
    And it is ever new;
The first and last of all the songs,
    For it is ever true;
A little song, a tender song,
    The only song it hath:
There was a youth of Ascalon
    Who loved a girl of Gath."

From *Once on a Time*
by Kendall Banning.

Contents

Chapter One

Some of the Girls

This is going to be a book about you and the men in your life . . . a primer of *do's* and *don'ts* . . . of how to make men, and impress women. How to make a lobster newburg, and some very swell canapés. How to dress . . . how to decorate. How to have a party on a shoe string . . . and raise an orchid in the kitchen. And how to fix a room (any old room), so as to make everybody who steps into it happy—including yourself.

Life is fun, if you can take it. But pleasant things and lovely things do not happen often enough of their own accord. And every-day living goes flat, if

1

you leave it alone. Life is too short for us to bore ourselves. And to find happiness you must work for it.

There are recipes in this little book for joy, content and cocktails . . . formulas for living and loving—and a fool-proof way to make a rabbit. How to cook for fun—and how to drink, and not be sorry. When to be giving, and when to be wise. How to get a man—and how to lose him.

*   *   *

Girls who are successes in the Love Dept. were not born with mink coats on their backs. Consider the women who have arrived where you'd like to be. Their backgrounds were seldom spring boards to riches or stardom. Many of them started at scratch, and determination got them places.

Beauty is a help, and lovely legs will take a girl a long way. But wisdom is better than rubies, plus anything else you can think of. And don't let anyone tell you that brains don't count—or that it doesn't pay to be nice.

We are all out there, plugging away at trying to get the most out of life. And there's no reason why any smart girl should hang around waiting for the telephone to ring . . . not if she'll study this *Guide To Happiness,* learn a few trade secrets, and get in a little home work.

Sitting alone nights may develop the philosopher in you, and comfort for your old age. But the philosopher in you is nothing to waste a summer night on—not if you've a heart to love, and lips to kiss with.

* * *

Jerry Weidman (a good-looking bachelor who writes books) says that all normal girls want to get married. The girls who don't are either hopelessly mad, or they are lying in their teeth (sez Jerry) . . . But any girl can get married, if she feels that way about it—with all the men there are around!

So draw up your chairs, my little ones. . . .

We are not going to guarantee—if you read this book from cover to cover—that you will have beautiful young men fainting on your door step. But we do promise that you will have more good times. We believe that, being a girl, you should make the best of it, and get some fun out of it. Personally, we're no heart breaker—as we are practically the first to admit—but we have been around, with both eyes open—and our two little ears . . . and much have we seen and heard.

* * *

Once upon a time, when I was in the seventh grade, I had a teacher whom we will call Miss Minnie Dunks. You could tell to look at Miss

Minnie the life she'd led, for she had a mole on her nose and a cast in her eye. And she used to write a sentence on the board, for sinners to copy. In a fine and flowing hand she wrote it:

I would rather be respected than loved.

That sentence, reflecting Miss Minnie's life, conditioned mine. Ten times—twenty times—*fifty* times —day after day, I copied it. Until, in a grim, precocious way, I got a juvenile malaise, and muttered in my middy-tie:

"The hell I would!"

*   *   *

Then there was grandmother. Grandmother was a little girl in Ireland when the Good Queen busied herself setting godly standards for the Empire. Grandmother got a bad case of Victorianism, and brought it over from Dublin.

"Be good, sweet maid," said Grandma. "Be good, sweet maid, and let who will be clever."

Although I was but a wee colleen, I was smarter than that. For what did goodness ever get Grandma? Obviously Grandpa. And Grandpa was no Omar Khayyam.

A book of verses . . . a jug of wine, a loaf of bread, and thou . . . beside me, singing in the wilderness. . . .

After the Rubaiyat, I discovered Laurence Hope. . . .

> *Pale hands I loved beside the Shalimar . . .*
> *Where are you now?*

I settled on specifications for a future husband, the ideal man. He must be six feet tall, dark and handsome, with piercing black eyes, and broad shoulders. He must dance divinely, play the guitar, and sing in a wonderful bass. He would call me *Chiquita,* and we would go to a Dude Ranch on our honeymoon.

> *Hot sands burning fire my veins with passion bold.*
> *Love me—I'll love thee . . . 'til the sands of the*
> *desert grow cold. . . .*

When Grandma found me memorizing Swinburne, she said an extra rosary.

> *O sad kissed mouth, how sorrowful it is! . . .*
> *To have known love, how bitter a thing it is.*

Then there was Edna St. Vincent Millay:

> *My candle burns at both ends,*
> *It will not last the night;*
> *But ah, my foes, and oh, my friends—*
> *It gives a lovely light!*

After that I got to be a reporter. Teacher and Grandmother were in their sainted graves—and on I went, from bad to worse.

Being a reporter was a bed of roses. Heaven lay about me. And hussies, I noticed, were happy as saints.

I interviewed Walter (*Life Begins at Forty*) Pitkin, the late Florenz Ziegfeld, Jack Dempsey, President Coolidge, and Babe Ruth. I asked their various opinions of American women,—and what did they think of petting? I was working for Mr. Hearst at the time, and those were standard questions in the best tabloid tradition.

Then one day I was sent to interview Gamaliel Bradford, a quiet and scholarly gentleman whose *psychographs* had thrilled the literate world. *Psychograph* was a word invented by Mr. Bradford, who had explored the loves of history's handmaidens, and written with gentle understanding of their lives and amours. The title of his new book was *Daughters of Eve.** And it was a collection of spiritual biographies, or *soul portraits,* of women beloved by many men.

My outrageous assignment was to ask Mr. Bradford how the ladies got that way, and to analyze for our readers the secrets of their amorous success . . . to tell us how Eve's daughters enchanted men— how they got them, and how they kept them.

Mr. Bradford was kind and helpful. He told me about Ninon de Lenclos, and Sarah Bernhardt,

* Houghton Mifflin.

about Catherine the Great, and the poor little goose girl who married the greatest king in the world. What he told me made such good copy that I sold a syndicated newspaper piece that ran on two pages —with a photograph of Mr. Bradford on one side, and George Sand wearing pants on the other.

When it was published, Mr. Bradford wrote me an amused little letter, suggesting that one day I should develop the subject, and write a book of my own. Which is exactly what I am going to do. And if you pattern on the dispositions (but *not* the morals!) of these loved and loving ladies, you will have beaux to spare—and husbands for the choosing.

Mr. Bradford had a theory that every girl can profit by. For success in love, women should thoughtfully make life a fine art. And he spoke of Ninon de Lenclos, who did it instinctively.

Ninon was born in Paris the year the Pilgrims came to America, and became the adored scandal of the age. Some of the greatest men were her lovers; the most interesting women her friends.

She was such a girl, declared Mr. Bradford, as America breeds today. Fearing neither hell nor high water, she dared everything. She was determined to get from life every drop of sweetness it could yield. And—getting it—she got away with it.

Ninon seemed always joyous, and never grew old. She had the tremendous energy and glowing happiness that goes with vitality and radiant health. It was said that a mysterious old man in a black cloak furnished her with magic pills. But maybe Ninon just knew about vitamins and minerals.*

Sex played a showy and conspicuous part in Ninon's career—and played it to the end. It was said that she charmed the Sévignés of three generations. And the Abbé Gédoyn made love to her when she was eighty.

The saving thing about Ninon was the common sense that kept her head steady through the madness of her girlhood, and carried her to an old age of dignity. You would have thought such a woman would have a sordid and horrid end. Yet Ninon had the admiration and respect of the very best people.

"But there is not a girl in a thousand who could do what Ninon did, and end as she did," said Mr. Bradford. "Few women would have the sanity and sense—and calm vision of future possibilities—to steer through so many perils to a port of peace."

A very consoling thing about Ninon is that she was not beautiful. Her loveliest quality was her sweet good nature. She loved mirth, and identified

---

* *The U. S. Government recommends a pint of milk a day and Vitamin C for sex appeal, plus meat and an egg—and two vegetables (green and yellow).*

love with laughter and gaiety. And her voice was as merry and sweet as a brook.

Listen to your own voice. If it is whiney, get some life and lilt into it, because the telephone gives a girl away these days. And a thin, listless tone will make a man think you are as old and unhappy as Madame X. While a vibrant voice will make him want to date you.

Ninon never reproached men, or nagged them, or tried to make them over. And she was always ready to let go. . . .

> For *this is Wisdom; to love, to live,*
> *To take what Fate, or the Gods, may give.*
> *To ask no question, to make no prayer,*
> *To kiss the lips, and caress the hair.*
> *To speed passion's ebb as you greet its flow*
> *To have,—to hold,—and,—in time,—let go!*

Ninon let go without desperation or reproach— nor tried to cling to an out-worn love. And she was never, *never* bitter!

Her vast experience had taught her, or she thought it had, that a man's passion is brief, however ardent —and the more ardent, the briefer.

When men tire, some broody little girls love to anguish. But Ninon was no lily-livered lass. She dared take love as it offered.

And when it was over, Ninon remembered with exultation that she had had what no coward could.

"You should taste love," she said, "and savor it, and fling it away, and forget it. Otherwise, you run the extreme risk of being flung away and forgotten yourself."

Ninon is said never to have betrayed a confidence, or slandered a friend. She loved charming gossip, but despised unkindness. And her daily prayer was:

"Dear God, make me a good man,—but NEVER a good woman!"

She kept her word, paid her bills, and usually told the truth.

She rarely touched alcohol, and with her natural vivacity she didn't need to. And she abhorred a drunkard.

What drew people to Ninon besides her loyalty and amiability, was her spontaneous appreciation and enjoyment of life. They knew that beneath her mirth and laughter, lay tenderness and understanding.

"I believe I go further than most people," said Ninon, "in everything that touches the heart."

"And that," said Mr. Bradford, "was the secret of her success. She touched hearts because she loved them, because she turned to them with sympathetic curiosity, and handled them with a gentle and affectionate touch."

*   *   *

Madame de Maintenon was different from Ninon, and she was not pretty either. In fact, she was homely. But she, too, had a sensible head on her shoulders—and a great desire to get what she wanted.

She was a poor little girl who tended geese, and married a paralytic poet to escape poverty. After his death, she determinedly made powerful friends, and fought her way up until she met the *King,* no less! —Louis XIV. She charmed him, as she did everybody else, and he persuaded her to take charge of his illegitimate children.

Then Louis abandoned all other loves, and made Madame a Marquise—and practically a Queen. And for thirty years she maintained her position with gentle dignity. She had begun life in poverty and misery. Now she was at the top. And it was charm that got her there.

Maintenon was prettily, efficiently domestic. At Versailles she sometimes went into the kitchen, put on an apron, and cooked.

And if anyone objected that she would smell of onions in the parlour, she laughed and said, "That's all right. They will not believe it is I."

She was distinguished for her tact and sympathy. But her success with the King was largely due to her consuming desire to please.

"I have never seen anyone like me in that respect,"

she said. "I was sensitive to the praises of the King, and I was just as sensitive to those of a laborer. There was nothing I should not have been capable of doing or suffering to get well spoken of."

When the King passed on, Maintenon went to a convent and died, as they say, in the odor of sanctity.

In her very old age, smiling on a little nun, she said "God has given me grace, ma chérie, to please everybody."

"And God knows," she might have added, "I've worked at it!"

*   *   *

When Russia was the greatest Empire in the world, Catherine the Great sat upon the throne—and Catherine had more lovers than any Queen should. Her latest biographer says there were fifteen. But mathematical precision is not important. It was the personality of the Queen that interested Mr. Bradford.

"She was a normal, substantial, working woman," he said, "with a healthy human merriment. She loved a good time, had a feminine appreciation of a handsome man—and had the handsomest men in the world at her disposal."

She was thoroughly a woman in the ordinary, domestic concerns of living. And like many a glamour girl, Catherine was quite at home in the kitchen.

"She was immensely generous," said Mr. Bradford. "Yet in giving—as in living and loving—she kept her head. She spent, she lavished—yet she never really squandered. And she had the vital instinct of always wanting to see where the money was coming from, before she let it go."

When Catherine went to Saint Petersburg, at the invitation of the Empress, to marry the heir to the Russian Empire, she had only six panties to her name, three dresses, and half a dozen pairs of stockings. The Czarina, who wangled the match, had *15,000* dresses and *5,000* pairs of shoes. And no wonder Catherine felt like Orphan Annie.

Catherine liked people, liked to be with them, to study them, and to please them. She was a great listener, and a great questioner.

"A large part of the secret of her success was a fresh and exuberant delight in living," said Mr. Bradford, "and a philosophy that excluded worry."

"*Worry,*" Catherine said, "*is a mean, avoidable and disgraceful disease.*". . . And she kept her looks, because she meant it.

The Empress was a party girl. But she was a determined party girl, and enormously ambitious. She achieved self-improvement through reading, and a system I will tell you about later.

"In my view," she said, "the one who goes ahead is always the one who wins."

And Catherine kept going. She took lovers, and waged wars—and for thirty years, kept herself on the perilous golden throne of Russia.

*   *   *

A widow I know—poor as a church mouse—and as determined and ambitious, in her own little way, as the Empress, adopted a motto like Catherine's. And went ahead and won—a fabulously rich husband!

The widow wanted to get married—not to anyone —but to someone Very Special. Budgets were the Cross she bore, and pinching pennies was her purgatory. So she planned a carefully calculated campaign, and gambled for big stakes.

On borrowed money, she moved into a small, select hotel. She furnished a suite with extremely elegant furniture, rented from another impoverished widow; and there she gave small, correct dinners. She entertained discreetly; and by being always amiable, always amenable, wangled week-end invitations, and kept herself in circulation. Until, by and by, she met a rich and lonely widower, who thought she was perfectly wonderful, and proposed over the demi-tasse and grand marnier the first night she had him alone for dinner.

This stalking and gunning business is not recommended for jeunes filles. Rich old widowers are fair game for desperate widows—but it's more fun to be a young man's werling than an old man's derling.* And the anecdote of the determined widow merely bears out the Empress' contention that *the one who goes ahead is always the one who wins.*

*   *   *

Sarah Bernhardt had a very modern motto— *Quand même—Even if . . . So what? . . .* No matter. Take the best of life, and eat it with both hands. Take it sweet, and full of beauty and splendor. Make a riot of it, and a revel. And if disaster comes, and misery—and crooked Fortune smiles her spitefulest—you will have had your hour. Had it, and loved it. *So what?*

You wouldn't remember Bernhardt, my little ones. She came to America on a fabulous Farewell Tour —with a wooden leg, and a coffin. We went from school to see her—and laughed and cried. And waited at the stage door, to catch a glimpse of her in a leopard coat and a crutch—with orchids on her shoulder, and her mouth like a bleeding gash in a face like wax.

* *Proverbes* of John Heywood (1546).

Bernhardt had one husband, a number of lovers, a son Maurice, and whatever it takes. . . . In New England, we call it *gumption* . . . and the old folks called it *spunk*.

"Put your best foot forward," Grandma used to say, "and have a little spunk about you!"

"What carried Sarah Bernhardt to triumphant consummation," said Mr. Bradford, "was the magnificent, vital energy and persistence of her character. You could not discourage her, or dishearten her . . . or beat her, or kill her."

In the early days she said to George Sand, "Madame, I would rather die than not be the greatest actress in the world."

She was nine, when she adopted her reckless motto—*Quand même*. Her young cousin had challenged her to jump a ditch, and she had fallen, broken her wrist, and bruised her whole body. And when they carried her home, she shouted:

"I will do it again! If he dares me, I will do it again. And I will *always* do what I want to do!"

Psychologists call this the *courageous approach to life*. And Grandma called it *guts*.

Quand même . . . *Quand même* . . . If you haven't a touch of *quand même,* you should go out and get some. For life is not life without delight. And to get out of it the best there is in it, a girl must gamble.

He fears his fate too much,
  Or his deserts are small,
Who dares not put it to the touch,
  To gain or lose it all.

That verse was written by a man who lived in Shakespeare's time—James Graham, the first Marquis of Montrose. Mr. Bradford quoted it as an appropriate theme song for glamour girls. But I know braver lines than those—and if you would like something superb to blaze on your escutcheon, here you are:

Henceforth I ask not good fortune.
I myself am Good Fortune.

The will-to-triumph is half the battle . . . and ability is the other half. But the clever girl hides her battle ax and camouflages her armor—and, *knowing she is Good Fortune,* wears her charm on her sleeve!

Chapter Two

The Men in Your Life

Some people think charm is a mysterious attribute. As a matter of fact, it is any number of things—and most of them pretty obvious.

James (*What Every Woman Knows*) Barrie said, "If you have it, you don't need to have anything else. If you haven't it, it doesn't matter what else you have."

But that is just a neat little bromide. And no girl is exempt from romance and glamour.

18

Some women have an instinctive faculty for pleasing men. And some have to work at it. But don't break your neck! Nothing is sadder than the terrible sight of a girl with darn little charm working at it like crazy.

God was good to some girls, and has indubitably bestowed His bounty on the undeserving. While many a good child says her prayers, and hopes for the best. . . . But now comes an answer to the maiden's prayers—a list of *do's* and *don'ts* . . . what men like, and what they don't like.

Judging from the conversation of the men I know, there are many things they dislike in women (or maybe it's only in me). They don't like us cute. They don't like us dull. They want a girl who can talk. But never a long-winded story! They hate explanations, and abominate apologies. . . . But keep a man waiting without a darn good reason, and see what you get! They like us smart, and they want us smooth.

Men (even exhibitionists) hate to have the girl they're squiring attract unfavorable attention—and especially in restaurants. Most men think a girl is feeble-minded who always laughs, screams, and makes a large noise in public. On the other hand, you've got to laugh at their little sallies, or they *know* you're dumb.

They hate to have us drop our bags, our gloves, or

our lipsticks. They can't understand the way our laps are slippery, or why we forget like we do when we stand up.

They cannot bear to have us bawl out waiters, or be audibly sarcastic about food or service. They don't want us to send back cold soup, mutter over dehydrated steak . . . or even protest a luke-warm Martini.

Speaking of drinks, most men flinch to see a woman make hash of an Old Fashioned. A muddler's no plaything, they say—and that stick of pineapple wasn't meant for marmalade.

Some girls think it's cute to order "one of those drinks with a cherry in it"—or that "pretty pink one." This may make a hit with an aging escort, but is apt to make the waiter slightly sick (in case you care). And, unless you are the pixy type—but *definitely!*—or under sixteen, call a Manhattan a *Manhattan,* and leave a Pink Lady alone.

A good way to alienate men is by being possessive. Where women are concerned, men have to be led—and never, *never* driven. Possessiveness panics the boys. And when a girl asserts her *right* to a man's love, she kills it.

Men resent any sort of compulsion, and especially compulsion of their affections. You can't make a man love you, or want to belong to you. And there's no use trying.

Men like attention, but resent domination. Don't clutch a man—or grab, or paw. Don't hang on to his arm, or hold his hand. Or lean against his manly chest (I'm talking about in public).

When I was small, my grandfather used to say, "Look at things all you've a mind to—but *don't touch!*"

What Grandpa had in mind was something breakable. But it's a good idea anyhow. Even women hate to see a woman touch a man. It's bad manners. . . . And—speaking of manners—did you hear about the reporter in Oklahoma City who performed 124 polite acts toward women, and was thanked only twice?

He wrote a piece for the paper, and the men fumed with indignation. They say we take their gallantry for granted. And that we don't listen when we're spoken to. (I think they mean that we let our attention wander when they bore us.)

Inattention hurts a man's ego, and a lot of it will give him an inferior feeling. In large doses, inattention leads to the divorce court—and an attentive woman's arms.

Men like to be thanked for small favors. And they don't like it if we take their courtesies and attentions for granted. Be grateful, but don't gush. And *don't* be cute!

Be yourself—your *best* self, of course. Try to make

people happy, and be a little kinder than is necessary.

There was a man whose wife criticized everything he did, and compared him unfavorably with all the men of their acquaintance. Until he felt about as big as a midge, and fell in love with someone else.

When he asked for a divorce, his wife raved and ranted.

"The so-and-so, and so-and-so. . . . I'll bet she *flattered* you!"

But the wife didn't—and she wouldn't. . . . And so she lost him.

What every woman knows, and too few remember, is that it is a mistake to nag. If you want a sure-fire technique to make a man scram like you were Typhoid Mary, remind him not to forget, ask him *did he, will he*—well, *why didn't he?* Men will go practically anywhere to escape nagging—and some of them never come back.

If you are the maternal type, don't go overboard. Men like a little gentle mothering—*"Poor, darling—don't work too hard!"* . . . They will even let you get their rubbers . . . and remind them that coffee keeps them awake nights. But don't tell them when they've had one drink too many. Or that everybody's heard that one before.

Men are more self-conscious than women. And many of them are old-fashioned about "nice girls" (the quaint darlings!) There are women who won't believe this, but men don't like girls to tell dirty stories, or talk like truck drivers.

Men are fastidious. It bothers them to see a girl sit awkwardly. They've noticed that horrid little way we yank down our girdles. They disapprove of many of our clothes . . . principally our slacks—unless we are built like Marlene Dietrich. They say that a woman in pants looks like a drunken dollar mark—and some of them say worse than that. They also say that bare legs aren't half as good looking as we seem to think they are—and, as a matter of fact, they *aren't*.

They object to too-low evening things, and too-short swimming things. Scanty costumes appeal to a man when it is the right time, the right place, and the right girl. But most men like the special privilege feeling. And they don't get it on a dance floor, or at Jones Beach.

Men like nice round bosoms, nice round hips, and nice pretty legs. But they are not nearly so critical of our figures as they might be, if they were a little smarter. And if your figure has not the lines you'd have picked, you can get the right sort of scenery for camouflage.

Men want their girls to look smart. But most of them dislike freaky clothes and extravagant make-up. They prefer red lipstick to purple or orange—and they wish we wouldn't put it on just before they kiss us.

They hate to have us talk about their friends . . . or talk too long about anything. If you are telling a story, and see a man's interest flagging—stop! Start another—or just shut up. It takes most women a notoriously long time to tell a story. A good rule is to get to the point first—and embellish afterward.

Fat women talk too much about their diets. Talk too much, and do too little. A soft sister on a stool at Schrafft's, gobbling a double-fudge marshmallow sundae is a horrid sight. And nobody wants to hear her talk about calories over clear soup at dinnertime.

On the other hand, men have an aversion for girls who play with shredded lettuce. Bird-like appetites frighten them. And the girl who always picks at food sometimes scares away a lusty lover.

Men say we ponder menus like they were Christmas lists.

If they try to be helpful and say, *"What about a nice plank steak?"* We say, *"Where do you see plank steak?"*

And not until we've seen it with our own two eyes, are we satisfied. After which we say we guess we'll have the baked stuffed lobster—or a seafood salad, maybe.

Men would change us, if they could. Make us more reasonable, for one thing. Less suspicious, for another. But they hardly ever try.

It is women who are the makers-over. Reformation is a female passion. And where does it lead? Down a nasty blind alley with nothing at the end but loneliness. And the bread spoiled, and the wine spilled!

If there are a lot of things you don't like about a man, forget him . . . or try to. Anyhow, don't try to make him over. Take him as he is—take him . . . or leave him.

*　　*　　*

The greatest game in the world is the game between men and women.

"Sex," as some high-class thinker remarked, "is bearable, though it will continue to be irrational, and a great nuisance." . . . In other words, sex is a problem—but it's a swell one.

> *Woman more love than man doth feel,*
> *Yet mad with love, must love conceal.*

A clever girl keeps a man hotly hopeful, and runs away to make him chase her—tantalizing to the point where he pursues, begs, and promises. He will give her anything, if only she will love him. So the woman charms—the man succumbs. . . .

And then it's hell the way the chasing changes. In the beginning of a love affair, the man is the maker of occasions. But at the end, it is the woman. And when the chase goes into reverse, it's ashes in our hair.

*   *   *

A lot of girls make the mistake of telling their best friends that they are practically engaged—on a couple of dates and a soda. If a man thinks you are trying to marry him, you will have a tough time doing it. But keep your head, and watch your step. And you can get married, if you want to.

A girl can tell when a proposal is coming. If she isn't going to grab it, she should duck it, and never boast of conquests. But close her mouth, and save the boys their dignity.

And remember that men don't like phonies. Even the phonies don't like phonies.

In the West Indies, when a girl wants a lover, she buys some *temptin' poudre,* and puts the evil eye on the rest of the girls. And if she wants him to marry her, she burns a candle upside down, and prays to the Devil. Such marriages do not work out very well, because *obeah* is bad business. But then neither do all of those established with the benediction of the Almighty. Three out of four American marriages are unsuccessful, and the average duration of marital happiness (blessed by God and State) is less than four years.

I had a cook in the West Indies named Auxanges, which means *of the angels*. Auxanges led what was euphoniously known as the *sweet life*. She was a desirable and an amazingly desirous girl, who took her fun where she found it and kept her head, while she took it.

"Love am like a sickness," Auxanges told me. "Folkses get ovah it—but isstead of feelin' bettah, dey feels worse. . . . When a man finds out dat a 'oman is crazy about 'im, he don' crave dat 'oman no moah. An', Miss, don' youah never permission youahself to think on one man all de time, 'cause it will run youah crazy, ef it don' kill you—daid-daid-*daid*."

Chapter Three

Every Girl her own Svengali —

Angels call it heavenly joy,
Infernal torture the devils say,
And men? They call it—Love.

In *Twelfth Night* there was a clown who sang
some wise little songs . . . and one of them was
about grabbing time by the forelock:

What is love? 'Tis not hereafter.
  Present mirth hath present laughter,
What's to come is still unsure.
  In delay there lies no plenty,
Then come kiss me, Sweet-and-Twenty,
  Youth's a stuff will not endure.

Three hundred years later, along came Prof. Pitkin and said *Life Begins At 40.* Well maybe it does— *maybe.* Twenty today . . . and forty tomorrow. But some of the nicest things that ever happened to a girl are going to happen to you long before you're forty—or they'll never happen at all. So Gather ye rosebuds while ye may, as Mr. Herrick said to the Virgins. And let me tell you how to play Svengali.

First you will have to get yourself in the right frame of mind. For if you are not going to be co-operative, or at least open-minded, you might as well skip this chapter. Auto-suggestion is sound and practical. The trouble is that it is practiced almost exclusively by neurotics . . . and that's what's the matter with them.

Of course it would be swell if we all looked like Dorothy Lamour. But it isn't necessary. It isn't even advisable. Because look at Dorothy and the work she has, keeping up with herself. Pure beauty is frail and capricious. And sometimes it is pretty wearing.

Individuality is a more desirable commodity. And smartness is practically indestructible. Either of them will take a girl a long way, and together they are worth more than all the starry eyes and ruby lips the poets sing about. Being pretty is nice. But being stylish is smarter.

In your grandmother's day, a girl without a Gibson profile hadn't a chance. And the ballrooms were thick with wallflowers. When your mother was a girl, flappers were the rage this side of paradise. Flappers all wore jersey dresses with pleated skirts, bobbed their hair like Fiji islanders, and thought it was cute to be dumb. For everybody wanted to be like everybody else,—and to be different was very hell!

But now Fashion is come to the realization that all women are not the same. We are embarked on an era of rights for big blondes and peanut brunettes, for helpless honeys, tomboys, and Lana Turners.

It's *smart* to be different. And it's not what you've got. But what can you do with it?

The worst defect a girl can have is not the shape of her nose or the cut of her mouth. It is the size of her inferiority complex, and a large complex can make a girl hunch her shoulders, duck her head, and carry herself like Ellie Mae in Tobacco Road.

Hold your chin up, walk like a queen—and you'll appear forty per cent better-looking than you are. For it's all what a girl adds up to. And if you don't believe me—what about Bette Davis' poppy eyes, and Joan Crawford's big mouth? Sylvia Sidney's eyelids are heavy, and Hepburn has far-flung nostrils. Helen Hayes is no beauty, and Garbo's feet are *much* bigger than yours.

Most of the glamour girls are coping with defects. It's the *will-to-triumph* that keeps them going, that

flashes their names in neon lights, brings them romance, or makes them rich.

No girl need be as plain as she was made. But
many a woman who tries to conceal her flaws would
better study and utilize them.

In Hollywood, a make-up man sits you in a chair,
with your hair slicked back, and your face as bare as
a bone. Maybe he will discover a latent possibility.
But more probably he will seize upon your worst
point, and individualize and dramatize it until your
best friend wouldn't know you—thank goodness.
For if you can't be pretty, you might as well be interesting.

If you don't like your looks, change them. If your
skin is bad, buy a ready-made complexion in the
nearest drug store . . . and while you are using
it, read up on diets, and get a skin you'd love to
touch.

If your figure is bad, get a new one. With diet
and exercise, any girl can go stream-lined, or curved.
It's just which you like better—a flat little tummy, or
butterscotch pecan sundaes.

Then learn how to dress. Find out what you can
wear, and what you can't—the lines that flatter, and
the lines that libel. Choose colors that compliment
you instead of those that swear at you.

Don't always be the modest little girl in ginger-
bread brown, or the sports model in luggage tan.

One basic color is pretty dull. And nothing but navy is just too practical to be exciting.

Black can be svelte and sophisticated, but it should have good lines, and maybe some smart accessories. Errand girls in Paris wore black, and looked drab. But *grandes dames* wore it—and looked grand. It all depends . . . But I am going to write a chapter about Clothes pretty soon—so now we'll get on to something else—Emotions first—and then Morals.

* * *

Emotions are the most important part of you. More important even than your intelligence. And the most important thing about them is your control over them.

Emotional maturity has a great deal to do with your success in love, and in everything else. And emotional *immaturity* can darn near ruin you.

Emotionally immature persons are brats in their behavior, regardless of age or experience. They are sore-heads, tantrum-tossers and blusterers. Jealous people are usually brattish. And so are most girls of the pixy type, many of whom are winsome little numbers addicted to bestowing whimsical names upon inanimate objects.

Do you remember when Dorothy Parker reviewed books for *The New Yorker* and signed herself *Con-*

stant Reader . . . and how she started to review a book that was plugged with whimsey—and all of a sudden she stopped.

"At this point," she explained, "Constant Weader fwowed up."

Well, that is the way some men feel about our little pixy sisters.

Auxanges, that black girl I told you about, had a lover named Evard.

"Dat Evard!" she cried. "Evard he brag 'bout he will power . . . but dat man he ain't got nothin' but *won't* power!"

Auxanges could hardly write her name, and Evard was a school teacher. But she had an emotional maturity worth more than his schooling.

Auxanges did not bother with restraining her affections. "I *enjoys* to pleasure mahself," she said. But she had self control based on an understanding of human relationships, and she could handle people like a diplomat. She understood herself—and she understood others.

Do you remember the ladies in Washington who fought about their social precedence, and wouldn't go in for dinner until they got a ruling from the State Department? . . . Without emotional maturity a woman wastes energy in emotions that might take her places, if she kept them under control.

"Fokses ain't no moah grown-up dan what dey fights ovah," said Auxanges.

The usual standards for success are fame, power and money—security, perhaps, for a woman. But these are not really success. Success is reaching a goal that represents the best use of your natural aptitudes. And you cannot be truly successful without emotional maturity, because you cannot achieve the best of which you are capable—and at the same time act like a child.

An emotionally mature person considers what she does now in the light of what it will mean in the future. You remember what Mr. Bradford said about Ninon . . . about her sense and sanity—and how, with all her reckless gaiety, she never lost sight of future possibilities. Such a woman can keep the future present in the present (if you know what I mean), and never let her heart run away with her head. A beautifully co-ordinated person has a level head and a warm heart—and this is the combination a girl should strive for.

You can be a smart stenographer, or a swell copy writer—or you can be President of the United States —and still be a child in your emotions, and raise hob to get your own way. But if you are a stenographer or a copy writer, you will have considerable trouble getting away with it.

The best way to acquire emotional control is to

teach yourself to think with detachment. Associate with persons in whom you recognize this special maturity—if they will let you. And imitate them —if you can.

Chapter Four

For This is Wisdom

For some time I have had my friends under such scrutiny as would give a guinea pig the heebie-jeebies; and I have been cultivating a psychiatrist, who makes up questionnaires on people's Love Lives and solicits answers like Dr. Gallup.

Most of the girls I know get by pretty well with men. But most of the girls the psychiatrist knows do *not*—and all he hears is misery. He is a probing man, filled with inquisitiveness and tenderness. Recently he concluded a five-year study of 634 couples, happily and unhappily married. And now he is working on what he calls a *psychological yardstick*, with which to measure personality traits and behavior patterns. With this scientific yardstick, the Doctor can predict the probable success or failure of a marriage. And if everybody listened to him, hardly anybody would get married. Then, of course, we wouldn't have so many divorces—but we wouldn't have so many nice families either.

"Girls," he says, "are brought up to believe that their biggest job is to hook a man who will support them. They may have to work for a while. But it is all to the good, because employment gives them a chance to buy tempting bait, and angle in promising waters."

By *tempting bait* the Doctor means cock-eyed hats, and up-lift bras, and crimson lipsticks. And when he talks about *promising waters,* he means the girls hook their prospects in offices.

Well, it is a mistake to assume that most women like to work, or dislike being supported. Many of

them—though not in love with any particular man
—and plenty able to take care of themselves, regard
marriage as something to make, if able. Personally,
I think the girls are cuckoo—though some of them
do very well by themselves . . . And who am I to
talk?

Very few marriages between completely adult
men and women turn out badly. It is the kids who
didn't know what it was all about who wake up, and
are sorry.

Unless you are *truly in love*—unless you *terribly*
need a meal ticket—unless you are lonely beyond
words—you'd better stick around. Take time to be
choosey. Get yourself a job—a job with a future.
And fill your spare time with interesting things.

Maybe you are sick of hearing about hobbies, and
how much they'd do for you. But girls who never
have time to think about themselves (morbidly
speaking, I mean) never get neuroses, seldom get
low, and usually get happy. And when I say hobbies,
I don't mean porcelain horses, or china tea cups.

I mean the things that money can't buy—the
things you use for conversational fodder. Try making a hobby of history or biography, psychology, or
cooking, or traveling. Maybe you can't *really* travel,
but you can cover a good deal of country in books.
Read movie and play reviews—and, as often as you
can, go to the theatre. I know a man who reads the

reviews so religiously, you'd hardly know he hadn't been to all the best plays. This is a compromise amusement, and a good intellectual pastime. Go to free exhibits and the museums—and make the most of your public library.

Daily papers, magazines, and newspapers will teach you how to talk. And self-improvement through reading will make any girl interesting. Choose a limited period, or a single author, and say to yourself:

"I am going to learn about the Elizabethan Era . . . or the French Revolution . . . or the works of Ernest Hemingway" . . . and pretty soon you will know so many things, you'll be like the people in the encyclopedia ads.

Maybe you think a hobby has nothing to do with beauty. But it has. The variety of a girl's interests reflects itself in the vitality of her face, and there is something awfully successful about vitality.

Popularity depends not so much on charm, as preached by the Margery Wilson school. Or on goodness, as plugged by Grandma and her league. But on vitality. When I was a kid I used to go to the Dartmouth Winter Carnivals, and I remember it was always a girl with *joie de vivre* sticking out all over her who was chosen Queen.

That was back in the days of Ella Wheeler Wilcox, who was called the Poetess of Passion, and when I had scarlet fever I memorized an epic that began *Last night I roamed the city streets and smiled at men.* There was something in it about *the ancient sin in my young eyes,* and when I recited it to my night nurse, she gave me a triple bromide . . . But what I started to say was this—Mrs. Wilcox wrote a poem that is by way of being a classic:

> *Laugh, and the world laughs with you;*
>   *Weep, and you weep alone;*
> *For the sad old earth must borrow its mirth,*
>   *But has troubles enough of its own.*

A light-hearted girl is a joy forever (and a light-headed one is a pain for aye) . . . But, of course, different men like different types. And a little generalizing won't do us any harm. Anyhow, I want to tell you about Tawheada.

Tawheada was the belle of Cairo. And she weighed 300 pounds.

Arabs are not in the least interested in any women but heavy-weights. And Tawheada, by reason of her amiable obesity, was the most popular woman in Egypt. I met her one night at a party at Shepheard's Hotel, where she held my hand and murmured pityingly.

"Pauvre enfant! . . . Poor little one."

I was so thin, my dragoman explained . . . and I hadn't any husband.

Before leaving the States, I had interviewed Edná Wallace Hopper, the perennial flapper. And Edna, bouncing up and down on a hotel sofa, had proclaimed enthusiastically how she kept thin. Carrots, I think it was—carrots and shredded cabbage.

Now, I thought it would be a good idea to find out how Tawheada kept fat. My dragoman asked if he might take me to call, and Tawheada came back with an invitation to the wedding of a grand-niece.

Tawheada—and I should have told you before this —was 60 years old. She had skin like a young girl— firm and smooth—and beautiful red hair that shone like the burnished copper in the bazaars and it was as soft and smooth as a child's.

The niece was married that night near Gizeh, where the pyramids are, and we motored out in Tawheada's limousine. In her youth, Tawheada was in a harem. But later she married a merchant reputed to be the richest man in Cairo. Although he was a Moslem, he had no harem—only one wife, and four French mistresses, which was considered more fashionable.

When he married Tawheada, he was a widower and getting on, so he sent the mistresses packing, and settled down to monogamy. But even monogamy was too much for the old gentleman. And after a month of wedded bliss, he sighed a deep sigh and died in his sleep. Tawheada had observed the traditional period of mourning. And now she was back in circulation.

Driving out to Gizeh, she talked of her niece and the preparations for the wedding. Aunt Tawheada, I gathered, was footing the bills. The dragoman translated, and I got what I could.

For weeks the bride had sat in darkness, and taken mud baths to bleach herself. To get fat, she had eaten barley, honey, and little, roasted mice.

She came riding on a camel, in from the desert. And she had on as many clothes as an Eskimo. Gold necklaces swayed beneath the chiffons, and bracelets clicked on her bare, brown ankles.

Her groom met her, and took her to his house. At the door he broke an egg to insure fertility. And as he unwound his bride, he threw out her clothes, one by one, while the wedding guests cheered. . . . But we were talking about what men like in women —and I mentioned Tawheada to show that you never can tell.

Tawheada gave me the secret of her weight, which was mostly nuts. Egyptian nuts and honey—and all meats and vegetables cooked in oil.

She was an amiable person, and enormously easy-going. Tranquil serenity is a comforting quality. And though some men might prefer the more secular charms of little old Edna Wallace Hopper, I think at the end of a tough day at the office, the gentle ways of Tawheada would be more consoling than the metallic lures of a perennial pixy.

Tawheada's voice was ever soft, gentle and low— *an excellent thing in woman,* as Mr. Shakespeare once observed.

Reading the biographies of lovely women, one is impressed by the way men loved their voices. They said Bernhardt had a *voix d'or.* It was Maintenon's voice that charmed the King. And Ninon's was like the "music of little birds."

*   *   *

If you can't talk, acquire the art of being an absorbed listener. And make yourself agreeable to everyone with whom you come in contact. You remember what Maintenon said: "I was sensitive to the praises of the King, and I was *just as sensitive to those of a laborer. There was nothing I should not have been capable of doing or suffering to get well spoken of.*"

Somewhere I read that the Irish value the good opinion of the pigs in the streets, and—being Irish— I think it's true. Be ingratiating then. Be cheerful— if possible. Don't argue—much. Don't slander— ever. And *never* talk about your troubles.

People are attracted to you by your manner more than by your looks. Pretty ways are a big help. And men care less about what a girl says than the way she says it.

Chapter Five

He's Looking at You!

A girl's best bet is her get-up, and it is smarter to be chic than pretty. Girls who would have been considered downright homely in their mothers' day, mask themselves in handsome habiliments, slap on a whacky little hat and a crimson mouth—and knock the boys for a loop. Then it's love at first sight, and devil take the dowdy.

Men are quicker impressed by clothes than character. Hearts of gold lose out to hussies in sheath silhouettes. And if it ain't love, it might as well be.

Love at first sight is an offhand emotional wallop, often induced by pleasant scenery on a pleasing wench. Then a stylish ensemble is worth more than a pure heart, and a man's eye will propel him into marriage faster than his higher nature.

Presumably you choose your clothes to please the boys. If you don't, go to the foot of the class . . . and what's the matter with you? Women have been dressing for men since Eve toyed with leaves in the Garden of Eden, and—wondering how the darn things looked—made a hit with Adam.

Good style makes the most of our looks, and expresses our individual temperaments. The best-dressed women are not duplicates of one another, but are as different as possible—and copy cats should use discretion.

The Duchess of Windsor has a streamlined figure and a Duke's fortune. And the Duchess, who has set a number of styles in her time, goes for a dramatic simplicity that takes a lean clothes horse and a rich husband. She wouldn't be caught dead on the patio of Government House in one of the bouffant, cuddly little numbers that Billie Burke wore to charm Flo Ziegfeld—and wears to this day . . . because Billie Burke is a clothes horse of another color.

The Duchess is the glamorous sophisticate—Billie Burke the orchidaceous coquette. Imagine the Duchess in a pinafore . . . or Billie Burke in shorts! Clever women dress to dramatize their characters. And dull women ape the styles they set.

Joan Crawford has shoulders like Jack Dempsey
. . . and because May Zilch thinks Joan is swell
and longs to look like her, manufacturers launched
a vogue for wide shoulders . . . and pints-of-peanuts
wore pads like chorus men.

Marlene Dietrich has a svelte figure, long legs, and
a high *derrière*—so Marlene wore slacks . . . and
little fat girls with short legs and low-slung chassis
wore them too!

Elizabeth Hawes, who is a stickler for dressing to
type, addressed the Junior League in New York, and
said (as nearly as I can remember) something like
this:

"I want you to get some mental pictures, Girls.
First, picture a Tart . . . now a Lady . . . and now
a Southern Belle. Picture Queen Elizabeth . . . Mae
West . . . and a Champion Golfer. . . You see them
all in different clothes—because, without clothes, it
would be hard to identify them, wouldn't it?"

Well then, our clothes should express our per-
sonalities—our own . . . and nobody else's. They
should also reveal our best points, and disguise our
worst.

The kind of clothes you need depends upon where
you live, and how you live, and what you do with
your life. The worst mistake some of us make is
buying things we have no use for, because they are

bargains, or because something similar looked well on someone else.

Once, in Bermuda, I fell for a bulky tweed made in heaven (or maybe Scotland), for a big-boned, rangy Britisher—and me just the opposite! Another time, I bought a chartreuse evening gown (chartreuse being a color I hate), because it was marked down from $250 to $49.50—and why not, since nobody wanted it?

There is a girl I know who is a sucker for satin. She doesn't get around much at night, but a marked-down dinner dress that shimmers is too much for her.

"I can always make a nice little negligee of it," she says . . . and, so help me, she does. The money that girl spends on negligees that look as if they were thrown together with a pitchfork would keep her in something smart, and do her more good. At least she could wear them in public places.

Unless you have a good deal of money to spend, it is a mistake to buy things conspicuously colorful. In the first place, you won't be able to wear them often—unless you don't mind seeming always to turn up in the same outfit. In the second place, they won't go with the rest of your things, and you'll have to spend money matching up—or go around pieced like a crazy quilt.

One reason that black is so good is that most men

won't recognize it as the same old dress—or anyhow, they won't be sure. Not if you change the neckline occasionally, and wear different gadgets.

Black is like the little girl who had the little curl. When it is good, it is very, *very* good—and when it is bad, it is *horrid*. Cheap black looks rusty. It gets shiny, and it gets wrinkled.

Black and white is usually good, and it doesn't have to be expensive to look smart.

One good outfit is worth a dozen mistakes. And if you like a thing well enough, it won't be any penance if you have to wear it until it is worn out. The thing to do is to wait until you are sure. When you see something you *think* you like, think it over. Ask yourself a few questions: *Do I really need it? Is it right for the occasions where I will have to wear it? Does it do all anything CAN do for my figure?"*

Beware the "bargains" marked down because nobody wanted them. Stick, when you can, with the good old classics. And remember that with a good suit and a black crepe dress a girl can go almost anywhere.

Buy your things for more than one season, unless you are a Rockefeller, or one of the du Ponts. A well-tailored suit should last a long time. A tweed coat is practically indestructible. Smooth styles survive. And a good cloth coat is a better buy than a cheap fur one. Best's and Peck & Peck show the same shirtmakers every year. And a black dinner dress on good lines can go to parties till it's a rag.

Speaking of evening things—men like sheer, dreamy black, and softly flowing white. And, mostly, they have a preference for exquisitely feminine things. Many of them are suckers for blue—the clear shade that does things for your skin. If you are young enough, they'll like you in pink. They like materials splashed with red poppies and passionate purple dahlias. They like very bright colors . . . and also gentle ones. Most of them dislike strange off-shades, like chartreuse and mustard.

They like dresses that suggest daisy fields, and honeysuckle and moonlight—soft blues, dusky pinks, and creamy things. They adore diaphanous stuffs that flow and cling.

George Jean Nathan says that the most effective way a woman can dress is to dress like a poor country girl expensively. Most men like clothes that make a woman seem delicate, fragile and frail—because, by contrast, I suppose it makes them feel big, brave and virile. They like lace at our throats and wrists.

Breath-taking decolletages embarrass them, and they want to take a sock at the guy who looks down your neck.

They like bracelets, earrings, and necklaces, and velvet bands crossed over white skin. These suggest captivity, and a man's response to make-believe bonds is sure as shooting. Jeweled "dog collars" enchant them. And gold and silver chains at throat and wrist arouse the slumbering cave man . . . Pagan at night. . .

And in the morning, a touch of the farmer's daughter. On summer mornings, men admire crisp little ginghams and cottons, pert and very fresh.

In the winter, they like black—and dark shades, brightened with color, in touches or in splashes. They like geranium red, emerald green, and blue-violet—and the off-red shades of coral, raspberry and strawberry.

They prefer dressmaker suits to *tailleurs,* and soft fabrics to tweeds.

They like heart-shaped necklines, and cascades of ruffles, and the swish of a taffeta petticoat.

A group of critics stood outside a theatre on 45th Street. They had come out for a drink, and were standing in a huddle when, without one word on the subject, one by one, they turned to look at some-one. Not turning himself, one of them asked Robert Benchley what they would be looking at.

"Oh," said Benchley, not turning either, "could be a girl in a red and blue dress" . . . And it was.

Red and blue is always good, and men go for it like homing pigeons. When there is a war, both colors are high fashion, and fated to be mated. But keep away from chevrons, stripes, brass buttons, and military accessories. Avoid mannish things—shirts, belts and stiffly tailored suits, because men in uniform hate uniforms. English girls are complaining that they can't get dates unless they change to girly dresses.

Men like veils, in perfumed whiffs. Very few of them like all red hats. But most of them admire a dark hat with a sock of color on it—and it's all right if the sock is red. They like small and large hats, but dislike silly ones. They don't like to have us hide one eye, or our noses. They like flowers on a hat, or feathers and excitement.

There is little use in trying to convert a man to a woman's way of thinking about clothes. But there is wisdom in studying his masculine preferences, and selecting styles of which he approves.

Men are more self-conscious than most girls know. They would rather squire you under-dressed than over-dressed. And unless you've got a Hattie Carnegie or a Muriel King, they'd just as soon you weren't *too* conspicuous. Men don't like erratic things, unless they're tops . . . and monkey-business embarrasses them.

They like dresses that show up a girl's figure, but not too much. Most of them dislike extremely short skirts. They like pinched-in waists, fitted basques, and lingerie touches fresh as a daisy. They like jersey that clings. And at night, they like tight bodices and blooming, bouffant skirts.

They generally lean toward the romantic rather than the sophisticated. Many of them have an aversion to "fussy things," and accuse us of wearing "too much junk." Generally speaking, they are pretty conservative.

Contrary to what seems to be a general belief, most men do *not* like sheer, black silk stockings, but prefer flesh tones.

Men like perfumes, but prefer an alluring aura to a three-bell alarm. Perfume is meant to be upsetting, and the office is no place to try it out. The proper way to use scent is with an atomizer. To get an aura on the subtle side, spray yourself all over after your bath.

Speaking of baths, beauticians advocate Luxury, Glamour and Bubble Baths—and a Heaven-give-me-rest bath, in which a girl wastes thirty minutes, and a lot of sweet-smelling, expensive beauty preparations. Beauticians give short shrift to showers, because they want to sell stuff to dissolve in tubs. But the stuff doesn't dissolve—and you sit on it.

For a quick pick-me-up, take a shower, rub Epsom salts all over you, finish off with cool water, spray yourself with cologne—and the hell with bubbles.

*　　*　　*

Once, when I was very young, I went to Havana with my cousin Constance, who became very seasick. I was devoted at the time to a perfume—black as ink and very oily—that I imagined made me smell like Circe, with a touch of Semiramis—but Connie said it was what was making her sick, and if I used it again, she would throw it out the port hole. . . I did—and so did Constance. And that ended my career as a worldly and seductive adventuress, because the man who gave it to me had brought it from Egypt, in a bottle without a name. And I could never get any more.

I got the Circe complex when I was about twelve, and started sprinkling cinnamon in my hair, because it smelled pretty in Grandmother's pomander balls. Grandma used to stick oranges full of cloves, and roll them in cinnamon, and hang them in the closet. This was supposed to slay moths, and make her capes and bonnets smell nice.

I was very patient with my hair in those days, and used to brush it fifty times every morning, and at night. I think this was because my father told me that a woman's hair was her crowning glory. Mother could sit on hers, and I was probably jealous.

Since then, I have learned that many men have a fixation about a girl's hair, and all of them detest a slovenly hair-do. It is one thing they find hard to forgive, though they seldom talk about it.

Catherine of Russia is said to have kept her *perruquier* for more than three years in a cage in her bedroom, to prevent him from telling people she wore a wig.

I know a girl who directed a publicity and advertising campaign in New England, who had her hair dyed because it was getting gray—and it came out red. A lovely and surprising red, that enchanted everybody except the natives, who appointed a committee to take suitable action.

"Only hussies have red hair," they told her, "and you must let yours get gray, or dye it black, so that people will know you are a lady."

Men are supposed to dislike red nail polish, but you have probably noticed that the girls who use it don't stay home biting their cuticle.

When I asked men the grooming faults that bother them, they listed too much make-up, untidy hair, unsightly hands, and twisted seams.

"Every man talks about twisted seams," I said. "It's just a habit. I never saw a girl with twisted seams in my life."

"Then look at your own," one of them said. And he quoted Robert Burns:

> "Oh wad some power the giftie gie us
> To see oursels as others see us!
> It wad fra monie a blunder free us,
>   An' foolish notion."

Chapter Six

It's Where the Rainbow Ends.

I love the story in Hartzell Spence's book (*One Foot in Heaven*) about what his father said to the woman who didn't want her daughter to go to New York. Mr. Spence's father was a Nebraskan Methodist minister, and the lady wanted him to give her daughter a good talking-to.

"Think what might happen to Kitty in a New

55

York apartment!" exclaimed the perturbed parent.

"Think what might happen to Kitty in a Nebraskan haystack!" retorted Mr. Spence.

Now, you may not know how that worried mother felt. But you probably know how Kitty felt, and how she longed to get away from the Nebraskan nest, to flutter down Fifth Avenue and try her young wings on Broadway. I hope she made it, and got herself a job that made the old folks proud.

It is wonderful to be awfully young and start making a career—and fall in love, maybe, on the way. And find a flat and fix it up. But hardly anybody can start at scratch. We have to make the most of what we have, and buy what we can afford. Some of you live in furnished rooms, and some at home. And at home it is often tough going, for the best of mothers get in a rut and won't let a girl express herself.

I remember when I wanted to paint Grandmother's mahogany drop-leaf table a "nice green" for the garden, and Mother said *Over her dead body!* We never could see eye to eye on this decorating business. Daughter was I in my mother's house, mistress at last in my own. And Mother, thank God, hung onto the mahogany.

I know a girl named Marjory who lived in a furnished room, with walls the color of jaundice. And slept in a brass bed, with a yellow spread limp

as a meadow of buttercups. In the room was an old-
fashioned bureau and two terrible chairs, one of
ptomaine green and the other a nasty brown.

She took the place because it was convenient and—
as the landlady firmly said—*reasonable*. It was also
pretty awful.

Well, it was good enough to sleep in, Marjory told
herself—and home was only a place to lux your
panties.

But those poisonous chairs got her down, and the
bedstead kept her awake nights. She stood it from
September until Columbus Day, when the holiday
fell on a Thursday and the boss gave her Friday off.
Then in four days Marjory turned her little hell hole
into the gayest place in the Village. And now they
call it Seventh Heaven.

I remember a colored preacher saying to Auxanges,
after she'd had a tempestuous affair with the baker,
"Well, Auxanges, you've made your bed. Now you'll
have to sleep in it."

Auxanges replied, "When Ah don' likes mah bed,
Ah makes it ovah."

"If you don't like a thing," Marjory told herself
sternly, "make it over!"

A can of paint, chintz for curtains and slip covers,
and six and a half yards of monks cloth did the trick.

If the idea of making slip covers terrifies you, it
is probably because you think they should be neat

and tidy. But they shouldn't. They should be loose and careless, and all you need is a pattern.

The landlady's son toted out the bedstead, and Marjory set the springs on bricks that raised it about a foot from the floor. Then she had the monks cloth tailored into a box-pleated cover that turned the bed into a studio couch. The monks cloth was 39 cents a yard. And with three spools of thread and ten yards of green cording, the bill—including $3.50 for making—was only $6.63.*

There is a wide sill in Marjory's room that opens on the fire escape; and the window sill became her kitchenette, the fire escape her refrigerator. She bought a two-burner electric plate for $1.98, a sandwich grill for a dollar, a Dutch oven for 69 cents, and a Silex coffee maker.

Recently I had dinner with Marjory, and we had meat balls, with Delmonico potatoes—and brownies for dessert. I will give you the recipes later, but before you can cook dinner, you must have a place to cook it in. And I have a number of suggestions for making that place pretty.

Anyone who is going to buy even a stick of furniture should do some studying on the subject, and look around to see what other people are up to.

* I forgot to say that this included a cover for the bed pillow and for four small pillows, besides.

If you were going to buy a trousseau, you would read fashion magazines, and you wouldn't buy a flossy going-away suit, if you were honeymooning at Peckett's; formal evening gowns, if you couldn't wear them—or ski pants for the Ritz.

But girls who should know better, sometimes do the maddest things when it comes to furniture. I know a girl who inherited a little old farm house and bought a modernistic suite for the parlor!

Decorating is a fascinating subject, and one that everybody should know something about. It is an easy subject too, and with very little effort you can become quite knowing.

Begin by reading home-making magazines. Maybe you think *House and Garden* is published for the little woman with her man all hooked, and a place in the suburbs—and maybe it is. But the magazines, with their magnificent color illustrations and diversified articles, are a step in the right direction, and an education in themselves.

If you want to study period furniture, borrow books from the library, and compile notes. Make scrap books, and paste up clippings from furniture booklets and ads. Or get stout manilla envelopes, write on the outside the identification of what is inside—and stuff with clippings (this is my own system). Then if you need something to whet your appetite, and give you courage to go ahead and *do* things, get *It's Fun to Decorate* * by Dorothy Draper.

The day it was published I bought a copy, and when I wanted to look on something lovely, I'd open it to page 86, and feast my eyes on a Carrara glass coffee table, with Lowestoft bowls of Madonna lilies —and handsome chintz chairs on the side.

I'd say to myself, "Some day I am going to own things just as beautiful—or beautifuler, maybe. . . ." And I did—as a matter of fact, I *do*.

I wish you could see my marble-topped coffee table. It belonged to my grandmother—and in her day it was a monstrous thing with heavy walnut legs. Grandma had it in the parlor, with a practically life-size statue on it of Dante and Beatrice. When Grandma died, we carted it up to the attic—being one of those families that never throw things away.

I had the legs cut down, so that it stands 16 inches from the floor, and on one side I have two small chairs, one done in turquoise and the other in violet sateen; and on the other side a low love seat, covered in West Indies madras with stripes of hyacinth and raspberry. The table is so sturdy and staunch that we can park our feet on it, or spill our cocktails. When I want to dress it up, I cover it with a lovely tea cloth and then it seems quite elegant. . . But what I started to say was Mrs. Draper's book would do you a world of good.

* Doubleday Doran.

You should also visit museums that have "American wings" and replica rooms of historical periods. "Model homes" set up in department and furniture stores are interesting and helpful—although I never yet saw one I wanted to walk away with.

*   *   *

Mrs. Sprightly is a divorcee with a staggering alimony, who decided recently to have her drawing room "done." She called in the best decorators in town, and they did an elegant job in five fancy figures, with a white fur rug on a polished black floor, with quilted satins, and chromium, and crystal —and the costliest things all two of a kind—twin end-tables of rosewood, inlaid with mother-of-pearl; twin vases, and lamps with alabaster bases; twin cigarette boxes and ash trays . . . and Mrs. Sprightly was so impressed she got a twin complex. She has a fit if anyone separates the cigarette boxes, or puts an ash tray on the wrong table. And of course the place looks exactly like a furniture display.

You've got to *live* in a room to make it look right. And it won't look right unless it is comfortable. There should be easy chairs, out-size ash trays, and lights wherever lights are needed.

Reading lamps should have strong bulbs—75 watt is usually about right, although some people prefer 100—and landladies cling to 40. Three 25 watt bulbs do *not* equal one 75 watt—and if you think so, you're straining your eyes.

Speaking of lights, reminds me of an actor I knew who had 119 lamps in a three-room apartment, and musical gadgets all over the place—especially in the bathroom, where a rhumba blared forth when you sneaked in to powder your nose. The living room looked like Radio City on a bright night. There were so many small tables, there was no room for traffic. And one night the actor's wife, who wore watermelon satin pajamas, took a header into the phony fireplace and broke her nose. Moral: Don't have a lot of cluttery things around.

Most living rooms have small, fragile tables that clutter the scenery and serve no good purpose. One day I had a man come with a saw, and reduce all my teetering tables to a common, comfortable height. They are conveniently placed beside the low chairs (*their* legs were sawed too); and now when I entertain there are handy places for people to set things. You know how it is to try to hold a glass in one hand and a fork in the other—when someone gives you a cup of coffee to balance on your knee.

It is a good idea to look with a detached eye on everything you own, and ask yourself: Is it functional? (i.e.—does it serve the purpose for which it was made?). Is it good-looking? Is it in scale? (i.e.—does it go with the rest of the furnishings?)

Functional and *scale* are patois in the decorators' lingo.

* * *

I want to tell you about my apartment—but it is hard to describe the place you live in. You get wandering off on details about where this or that came from, and never get around to telling what the place *looks* like. . . So I am going to put in here an excerpt from a magazine piece that Lorna Slocombe wrote.

"I caught my first glimpse of Eleanor Early's apartment as I walked down the mall of Boston's dignified Commonwealth Avenue. A glance toward the rooftops, and my heart leapt up as I beheld, on the very tip-top of a white apartment house, a row of geraniums in bloom, brilliant red against the blue sky.

"Eleanor Early lives in a penthouse, with terrace gardens front and back. The drawing room is rich with color—violets, rosy reds, purply blues . . . all the hues of tropical flowers. And on the walls are great, splashy paintings of West Indies scenes, echoing every color in the room. On the floor is a huge oval rug the color of raspberries, and as big as a baseball diamond.

"Chairs and sofas are covered with rosy tinted madras—that fine woven cotton which the women of the Indies twist around their heads for turbans. One entire wall is of glass bricks, and a luxurious vine trails across it, vibrant and green in the glow of soft light.

"That day the faint fragrance of midsummer flowers filled the room. There were bowls of them everywhere—white and velvety purple petunias . . . and red roses.

"'Would you like to see the garden?' Eleanor Early asked, and we went out on to the back terrace. In gay boxes, the flowers were growing, and blowing softly in the breeze that moved across the rooftops. Up on top of the town, the air was fresh and sweet, and we were near to the sun.

"On the terrace floor was a little charcoal pot such as the West Indies natives use for cooking. Eleanor Early cooks steak over the blazing coals, island-fashion.

"Beyond the balcony's flower-covered parapet is a sweeping view of quaint Boston chimney pots, over to the curve that is the Charles River.

"Eleanor Early's kitchen has the special charm which belongs to the kitchens of people who love to cook. It is no streamlined apartment kitchenette, with everything shut away behind impersonal doors. Open shelves hold gay porcelain cannisters and spice boxes. There are pictures on the wall, and over the stove is a portrait of Auxanges, her beloved West

Indian cook. There is a whole shelf of cook books, and notebooks of recipes collected from all corners of the world.

"It is the apartment of a writer (books on every side, manuscripts piled on a table . . . that huge plum-lacquer desk, meant for work. . . .) It is the apartment of a woman (the colors—clear, bright, feminine. . . .) But most of all, with its souvenirs from everywhere, with its cook books, flowers, and constantly ringing phone—it is the apartment of a woman who loves color—and enjoys life."

Speaking of color, I have always chosen the loveliest ones I could find, and thrown them together like mad. My cautious friends, wondering why they don't swear, think I have been luckier than I deserve, but when I read Mrs. Draper's book I knew the answer. It is because I have always instinctively chosen clear colors—and clear colors, she says, have a natural affinity.

Mustards and chartreuse, brown, and all wishy-washy shades just turn my stomach, while purples and scarlet and clear bright blues make me unduly optimistic. The only bright color I don't like is orange. Orange makes me think of Tea Shoppes and pumpkin pie and Hallowe'en, and I don't like any of them. I am not especially fond of yellow, either, although Van Gogh said it was the color most pleasing to God. Personally, I imagine God prefers papal purple and singing crimson, because they would go better than yellow with His golden throne and the pearly gates.

When I was small, grown-ups had an unwholesome respect for "good neutral colors"—especially mud-puddle taupe.

"It goes with everything," they'd say. "Such a safe color. . . ." And it had no more individuality than a grave-stone!

The psychology of color is pretty important, I think. Haven't you noticed how people who wear grays and browns, in the more disconsolate tones, have the *muddiest* dispositions? You have seen tenements the color of poverty that housed people with gray faces, whose souls were also gray. And you must have felt that in their lives there was no such thing as wonder and splendor.

To revolutionize a commonplace room, all you need is a few smart touches—plus color, comfort, and some sort of proportion, or balance.

Speaking of comfort—there's a girl I know whose husband gave her a twelve-room house for a wedding present. In their bedroom was a big fireplace, and when she saw it she said, "Oh, fireplaces are such dirty things! I'll have it boarded up at once." . . . And she did . . . and they lived wretchedly ever after.

One pleasant thing about using a lot of color is that you can get a large and vivid effect for little money. Primitive design, "peasanty" china, bright cottons, and colored glass go happily together.

You can also do pretty well with old things. My desk that I adore came from a place where they sell second-hand office furniture. I needed a huge one, and I wanted something with Chippendale lines, and plenty of drawer space. The mahogany ones that I priced were several hundred dollars. I found a used oak, bigger, and as staunch as any of them, for $10. I had it painted a beautiful purple, like Concord grapes glowing in the sunshine, and all its little curlycues touched with gold. But some paints, I am sorry to say, do not have the right staying powers (you should check carefully on them), because now my desk is the color of a dusty eggplant. Buttercup-yellow turned mustard on me once—and bright blue walls grew dark and drab.

We had a child's commode at our house that stood on spindly legs like a top-heavy sand-piper. For years it languished in the attic, until the day I needed a filing cabinet. Then I sawed off the legs, and sub-stituted carved blocks that stood under a Chinese chest that looked better without them. A coat of raspberry-red and some bright new hardware made a handsome thing of that old commode, and now it looks too interesting for the life it leads.

We had a bow-legged mahogany table in the "front hall," and when center tables went out, we retired it to the attic. But if I ever have a place where I can use consoles on either side of a door, I am going to get that old table and cut it in two. Maybe I will bleach it.

A decorator told me the other day that bleached blond furniture has come to stay, so I asked her how to do it, and she said it was pretty tiresome but not difficult.

Buy a big can of varnish remover, a good bleach, and a piece of fine sandpaper, painters' steel wool, and some clear lacquer. First remove the old finish with the varnish remover. This used to be a fearful job; but now there are strong removers, and it is not so bad. Then sandpaper thoroughly, to open the pores of the wood, and allow the bleach to soak in. Apply the bleach and let it stand for some time. Sandpaper once more, and then paint with clear, colorless lacquer. Rub down with a piece of steel wool. And give the furniture a light coating of wax, rubbed to a gloss.

To improve the texture of the grain and emphasize the blond effect, get some white wood filler. After the bleach has been applied and dried, go over the surface with the filler. This last step is known as *pickling*.

Old-fashioned, heavily-framed mirrors are sometimes effective when their frames are treated in this fashion. But don't use more than a piece or two of this blond business, because too much might be ghastly.

Speaking of frames, I found several beautiful plaster ones—very rococo indeed—in a junk shop, and picked them up for a song. Some of them I have had painted white and touched with gold. The others have been gilded. In two of them I have paintings done by a West Indies artist, and in the others there are mirrors. . . Did you know that you can buy sheet mirror for only $1.75 a square foot? And there is nothing that will do more for a place than mirrors. They make a room look larger and brighter. And you can place them to reflect all your prettiest things.

Now that I have mentioned those paintings, let me tell you that if you use a number of colors, it is wise to pull them together somehow—and that is what the paintings do for my place. Every color in the apartment is reproduced in them. I sent the artist snips of my fabrics and daubs of the paints I used. And once when I ran out of samples, I sent him a cranberry that was the color of a book-case, and the shoulder strap from a purple slip that matched a sateen-covered chair.

The artist's name is Hugh Stollmeyer. He has come from Trinidad to New York. And if you would like to hear people rave about your possessions, you can commission him to do a painting for you.

There are more things I should like to tell you, but unless you have a rugged disposition, you may have had enough. If you are a little Minnie Milquetoast, it will do your soul good to read *It's Fun to Decorate*. And if you get by on a budget, you may be inspired by Mrs. Draper's tips on how to dress up old furniture.

I do not hold with everything Mrs. Draper has to say, but I think she has the least trammeled ideas of any decorator I know. She says if you have Oriental rugs, and don't like Oriental rugs, *you should dye them!* When Bostonians read that they were scandalized. But when Mrs. Draper came to speak to the Fashion Group, the luncheon was a sell-out, and all the shocked people crowded around like a rally. And when she told how to salvage monstrosities, they began to warm up.

"Sometimes," she said, "you can do better with old things than with new." And the audience applauded, because Bostonians love everything that's old.

Now I am reminded of a patchwork quilt a lady sent me for a present, when my *Island Patchwork* was published. It is the Morning Star pattern, in red, white and blue, and I think it is the most beautiful quilt I ever saw. I never wanted an old-fashioned

room before, but now I have started planning. I
am going to get a four-poster bed, with a snow-white
canopy and a flounce. I shall have a cherry-red
carpet, and a sky-blue ceiling. I'll have dead white
walls, and red chintz curtains, and a big wing chair.
And on the floor I'll have braided rugs of red, white
and blue. I think I'll have a fireplace . . . and maybe
I'll have a cat.

Chapter Seven

How Happy We Will Be

Entertaining should be fun, but mostly it isn't. Hostesses usually work too hard. If they just relaxed, their parties would go better.

It doesn't seem to make much difference the money you spend. The dullest parties I ever went to were the costliest, and some of the best cost the least. We have all had a grand time on a two dollar evening, and a terrible flop on a twenty dollar one.

The secret of successful entertaining is forethought, and this chapter is going to suggest a few ways of simplifying things. It will deal with amateur entertaining on the informal side, which is the only side I know anything about.

I have never given a large or formal party, and please God I never will. I wouldn't know about being grand and very proper, but I can sail with assurance through casual dinners and midnight suppers. And I could cook a bounteous breakfast and call it brunch, if I wanted to—only *brunch* is a word I dislike.

I never gave a fancy dress ball, or engaged a Tyrolean orchestra, or had Elsa Maxwell for bait. But I have cooked memorable meals in my time, and served good drinks. I have done it with my two white hands, at the end of a tough day. And everybody always has a good time, including myself—which is more than some hostesses can say for themselves.

A girl shouldn't work too hard. After all, you invite people to give them a good time—not to make them feel sorry for you. And if the hostess doesn't enjoy herself, her guests will be ashamed to.

To forestall the jitters, get things ready in advance. Letting the canapés burn while you try to squeeze the lemons is one way of getting off on the wrong foot—and sticking your head in a hot oven doesn't help any. If you have burned the hors d'oeuvres, the boys and girls would rather eat them, singed and scorched, than get a play-by-play account of how it happened.

Many a helpless little honey has learned the gastronomic route to a man's heart, and it's simple as ABC. But any party deserves planning. Plan it

hard, and take it easy. Do your work ahead of time, and be relaxed when the doorbell rings.

Unless you are terribly clever, you should not try to entertain more than six persons at a time. Four would be easier. And two, easiest . . . easiest, and most fun.

When you entertain a man alone, you can ask him to help—which he will love, if you ask him right.

"Now," you'll say, "you mix the cocktails, dear, because you mix them so well" (though there's nothing the matter with the way you mix them yourself). Or, "Taste this, darling—I don't know if there's enough pepper in it." And "Tell me, honey

—is the steak done?" . . . Of course you know more about seasoning than he does, and nobody can fool *you* on a steak. But *flattery,* as Auxanges used to say, *is heaven to de mens.*

If you must entertain a gang, a *smörgasbord* supper is probably least trouble—though spaghetti is cheaper. A good rule is to serve only such food as you are sure will be successful, because you have served it many times before.

I have said that a hostess shouldn't work too hard. And now I say that she shouldn't make other people work either. I have been to parties—and you have too—when the night was just a chore, with guessing games and charades, athletic contests and handcraft.

Contests revive my repressed inferiority, and make me feel like the dumb kid I used to be in kindergarten. When I was in kindergarten, the teacher wouldn't let me march with the others, because I couldn't keep step. And she wouldn't let me sing, because I couldn't carry a tune. This ostracism left a scar, and may explain why childish competitions at grown-up parties lacerate me. But I have noticed that other people dislike them too.

When a hostess whips out pads of paper and pencils, and announces brightly that she has a nice new game, I think of the nasty child I used to know who wouldn't play unless I played *her* game.

"Now I'm the mother," she would say, "and you

are the bad little girl." Or "I'm the circus rider, and you're the old white horse."

I don't like games at a party. I like to listen and I like to talk,—if the talk is intelligent. I like to eat, and I like to drink, and I think that the food and drinks should be good. I dislike parties that try too hard to be amusing. And most people, I think, feel about as I do.

A number of things are fun until they are overdone. I knew a girl who had a big house, and a huge kitchen with a lot of pots and pans, who thought men just love to cook. Well maybe they did (some of them)—at first. She bought a number of big aprons and some chefs' caps, and when she had a party she dressed the men up, and turned them into the kitchen. At first it was rather fun. But no man likes being domestic when it begins to seem like work.

Once I went to a *very grand* party where the hostess was a nervous wreck. Everything was timed and staged, with the little woman and her husband exchanging signals, and the butler and the maid swapping high signs. Nervous tension is a contagious thing. The jittery hostess spread the jitters. Nobody relaxed, and the meal was agony.

Psychologists tell us that there is such a thing as unconsciously inviting disaster. If you have read the Old Testament, you remember Job and how he said,

What I feared came upon me. When a girl is afraid she isn't having a good party, then she *isn't*. And Job had nothing on an apprehensive hostess.

Women whom men find charming are not intellectuals, or beauties—but the bright girls who make themselves interesting. And this isn't a tough job, if a girl goes at it right. Keeping up with the current magazines will give a woman conversational fodder for cocktails, and ammunition for a month of dinner parties.

Almost all charmers show off. But the smarties do it smoothly. Don't strain to impress. Girls who toil tirelessly at being clever show the effort in their faces. Tension gets into their voices, and the struggle sticks out all over them.

Most men like to know that a woman—however gay and brittle—carries in herself serenity and peace; that she is deeply rooted in life. Someone wrote a poem about a woman whose "arms were like a quiet street at night," and I guess you know what he meant.

Mabel, who is a girl on the serene side, never had much luck exciting men—but, Lordy, how she can mother! Men are often preoccupied with something they consider more important than love. Or sometimes they are getting over another girl. Then Mabel gets in her licks.

The mothering girl gets a vicarious satisfaction playing second fiddle. And since most men enjoy tenderness, the maternal touch is usually appreciated.

Don't try to be a *femme fatale,* and take advantage of the fact that men like you—or, one day, you'll get your come-uppance. Because sirens get on, like the rest of us. And there is nothing lonelier than a middle-aged Magdalene with no one to work on.

*   *   *

Some men are pretty dumb about understanding why some girls live alone and like it. Of course if you are a frigid model, they don't think anything about it. You could hang out a *Man Wanted* sign, and they'd never see it. But if you are the man's-girl type, then it's different.

A lot of men will take advantage of the apartment situation. They have a crazy idea that girls should be protected. And if you haven't someone around to protect you, they think you do it on purpose.

The best way to take care of this Dumb Male situation is not to broadcast your private affairs. You don't have to volunteer that you live alone, and keep open house for nuisances.

Auxanges, speaking of a friend, said, "Dat 'oman, she keep sheself to sheself."

Being remote—but not *too* remote!—tempts a man, who seldom resists temptation. While the always accessible girl soon bores a restless beau.

Men like to think, when making a conquest, that it's their own idea. And if you thought of it first, keep your fingers crossed.

Alas! How easily things go wrong!
A sigh too much, or a kiss too long,
And there follows a mist and a weeping rain,
And life is never the same again.

Acting eager has made spinsters of some awfully nice girls. Gushing petrifies most men, and embarrasses them all. It is sweet to be hospitable, but don't over-do it. Because bombarding a man with invitations is no way to get around.

The city is full of nice girls with their latchstrings out, and what does it get them? When a man gets in the habit of dropping around for a drink and a bite to eat, he is going to be of precious little use to you. And you had better suppress the hospitable side of your nature, and suggest some spaghetti at Joe's.

* * *

It is important, I think, to be able to entertain—and often money well spent to do it. But the girl who is a sucker for spongers would better put her money on her back.

A girl who can whizz up a nice little meal rates high with the boys. Men are deeply moved when the drinks aren't too sweet, and the steak is done to a turn. But dinner à deux is only dinner—and may or may not lead to better things.

Love is something the boys have to be made to work for. And the girl who lets herself in for a lot of entertaining and no reciprocity, is getting nowhere awfully fast.

Don't go for a man who needs someone to take care of him. What you need is someone to take care of you.

And don't get mixed up with a second-rate Casanova, or any tawdry Don Juan. A girl gets paid back in heartaches for the fun she has bringing a wandering lad to heel—and if the other girls couldn't keep him, probably no one can.

When a girl is awfully young, she thinks that falling in love is a marvelous adventure. But when she gets older, she discovers it is just an accident. And, having discovered it, she does it again—and again!

There isn't any use trying to tell people in love anything. Now that you are a big girl—big enough to buy this book—you know everything. I'd like to give you some advice about what to look for in a man. But you wouldn't listen—and I guess a girl's got to find out for herself anyhow. So you pick your man . . . and I'll try to tell you how to entertain him.

*   *   *

I suppose you know that some women are ill just because they live in dreary rooms, and haven't any fun. They never have anyone in for a drink, or even a cup of tea. Lack of cheer makes them dull, and then bitter. And pretty soon they have to have the doctor. Then, if they have money enough, they have a psycho-analyst—when all the time there is nothing the matter with them that falling in love wouldn't cure, or pleasant companionship help.

A girl who is always tired is never charming—and usually irritable. And she hardly ever has a beau, because men don't date dull girls.

Some people think that they are tired because they are over-worked. But fatigue seldom comes from over-work. It usually comes (unless a person is really ill) from hating a job, from frustration, or from boredom. Resentment wears a girl out quicker than typing or dictation—or quicker than washing dishes. And something pleasant to think about is the best antidote.

You've got to have unusual strength of character to plan a party when you are feeling desolate; but the good old party-feeling is a wonderful cure for what ails you.

* * *

We had an old Irish maid once—Maggie—who went visting one Sunday. By bus and shank's mare she reached her destination, spent the afternoon, and came home again. And never will I forget Maggie's indignation as she told us of the treatment she got from "that one."

"She niver asked me did I have a mouth on me!"

The Irish have a lovely habit of bearing gifts. My grandmother never made a call empty-handed, or permitted a guest to leave without a present—a piece of cake done up in a napkin, roses in the summer time—a buxom bouquet bound with ribbon grass—or eggs in a basket.

It was a pleasant thing to be offered a cup of tea and a bite to eat as soon as you stepped in the door at Grandma's. A hospitable-looking lass shaking a welcoming cocktail conveys the same warming sensation.

When you entertain, the fire should be lighted before your guests come, and the tea or cocktail table spread. Flowers add to the color of a room, and are a decorative way of spending a little money.

If your coffee table is in front of the sofa (if you have a sofa), it should be a trifle lower than the seat. Whatever other tables you have should be low and sturdy. A nest of unpainted tables is a good investment. Cut the legs down, and paint them for your color scheme—and be sure to get paint that will stand up under hot dishes and alcohol.

Grandmother had blue and white Canton china

(I guess everybody's grandmother had), and she had a red tablecloth. Beside the table, on the window sill, was a row of red geraniums. And the whole business looked very cheery—especially on a dark day. If you have blue and white china, try it some time on a tulip-red cloth with bunting-blue napkins —and for a center-piece get a potted red geranium. . . . I still have Grandmother's Canton soup tureen, and it is beautiful for flowers—and practical for a one-dish meal of chowder or stew.

* * *

Even a cocktail girl should have a tea set. Silver is loveliest, especially the ancestral kind. But very few people have it, and copper is nice too. Sprigged china is charming, and there are old English patterns that are delightful. Some people like peasanty ware, but I think tea things should be fragile.

The other day I bought a huge tea tray in a junk shop for a dollar—English tin, light as a feather. And I painted it strawberry—a lovely color with my lavender tea cups. My hot water kettle came from a junk shop too, and under its grime it was shiny as a new penny.

None of my china or silver matches, because it was cheaper to pick it up bit by bit—but even if I had a million dollars, I should prefer it that way. I mean I like variety.

One of the most convenient things I have is a little muffin stand, to tote around at tea-time. Englishmen call it a *curate's assistant,* and it cost twenty-five cents, second-hand and a bit battered. But now it is painted to match the new tray, and it is as attractive as it's useful.

English people, who invented the habit, usually serve just bread and butter for tea. But if you invite people especially, you should give them something nicer—sandwiches, cinnamon toast—and little cakes, perhaps; with lemon *and* cream for their tea.

The best cinnamon toast is made with thickish slices of toast, buttered *generously,* and sprinkled *lavishly* with a mixture of three parts sugar to one of cinnamon. You can toast the bread ahead of time, and get it ready to slide under the flame at the last minute.

*   *   *

A girl's apartment should be glistening, shiny clean. But you'd be surprised how things can get dirty, and the girl who lives with them never know. I sublet a place once from a woman who had nice things, and a flair for color. And I thought it was charming until I moved in, and discovered that the upholstered furniture was musty, and the rugs had never been cleaned, or the curtains aired.

The English understand these things better than we do, and keep up appearances on practically noth-

ing. In Jamaica, I lived in an old, down-at-the-heels
Great House where the furniture was quietly falling
to pieces. But the floors were waxed until you could
see yourself in them. And *every day* the brass was
polished, and *every piece* of silver! "If seven maids
with seven mops had Swept it for half a year," they
could never have kept the old place sweeter.

But if cleanliness is a virtue, it is also a bore. And
it is more fun to decorate a place than to dust it.
Then soft lights are a camouflage, and flowers are a
help.

Chapter Eight

It's the Little Things.

Flowers are like a romance . . . because you love them so, you know they cannot last—and because you know they cannot last, you love them more!

Flowers make everyone happy, including the Chinese.

If you want to be happy an hour, get intoxicated.
If you want to be happy three days, get married.
If you want to be happy eight days, kill a pig and eat it.
But if you want to be happy forever, become a gardener! *

* Chinese Proverb.

Now, I like flowers as much as anybody. But on gardening I don't hold with the Chinese. Weeding makes my back ache, fertilizer makes me sneeze—and the Garden Club Girls can have it.

Some women find in horticulture what others seek in love and prayer—and this is the song the ladies sing:

> *Unless my palm may press the soil,*
> *Unless my hand may pull the weed,*
> *Unless my brow be damp with toil,*
> *The garden is not mine indeed.*

Well, there are also two schools of thought on *that* subject. And I know—because I once had a sweet little garden, dears—and a gardener named William. And I was as rhapsodical about my rubrum and rhododendron as any of the Garden Girls. Until William went to work for the priest, to ring the Angelus and cultivate the canna . . . And I had to go on where William left off.

Then my brow was wet with horrid sweat. And I wished it were William's. My flowers withered on the vine—for William's palm. Not mine. And I knew how Arthur Guiterman felt when he wrote a song *Against Gardens:*

> *They that make gardens raise bugs;*
> *Mildew, phylloxera, slugs,*
> *Japanese beetles and weevils,*

Rusts and mysterious evils.
What do they get for their seeds?
Only unlimited weeds,
Cutworms and other plant-killers,
Aphids and green caterpillars.
Why waste the beautiful hours?
Go to your florist for flowers! *

Or try house plants.

*   *   *

There was a sunny bay window in my grand-mother's sitting room where plants bloomed all winter, and threw a web of fragrance through the house. Grandma cut nasturtiums and petunias from her garden, and rooted them in pickle jars. She took up zinnias and marigolds in the fall, and potted them in butter crocks. And when the days grew cold, she dug blue lobelia from the garden, and pots of sweet alyssum. When Grandma went to call, she brought home slips of begonia and other women's geraniums, to root in jelly tumblers on the window sill.

On the what-not over the sofa were pots of wandering jew, with leaves of silver and purple. Wandering jew didn't mind the dark,—but other plants, Grandmother said, loved the sunshine.

When I grew older, I remembered her sunny window with its blossoms, and determined to raise

* *The New Yorker.*

plants of my own. But I had no luck. And I decided that it was because Grandmother was Irish and had *green thumbs* that things bloomed for her. It was a long time before I learned that the true reason was her kitchen range, with its gentle warmth and bubbling pots. And the kettle that steamed all day.

Then I thought that if I couldn't have a window full of plants—well, anyhow I'd have a few. I-would choose them for their decorative effect and fragrance. I'd nurse them, sensibly, on the window sill—and scatter them, at night, about the room. A flowering primrose by the big blue chair—African violets against crimson curtains—philodendron flinging heart-shaped leaves.

I had a window that faced south, with a sill broad enough for red geraniums, purple petunias, fuchsia, heliotrope in little pots, and a begonia like Grandmother's. Above the great north window I swung a 15-foot bamboo pole, filled with philodendron, that cascaded to the sill where the African violets bloomed.

Plants are like animals. They must have food and water, air and sunshine. If they get more food (fertilizer) than is good for them, they will get sick. And lack of water kills them quicker than anything else. They dislike drafts, and respond to tonics.*

* *Vigoro* is excellent.

You can get a special electric light bulb, and make them think it's sunshine. And humidifiers from the five-and-ten, to make the air moist. The reason why plants thrive in barber shops and at the hair dresser's is they get a load of moisture.

The easiest of all things to grow is philodendron, which waxes green in soil or water. And next to philodendron comes orchids.

An orchid is as tough as it is beautiful, and the only way to kill it is to give it too much water. For $3 (and up) you can buy a *Cypripedium* * (a Lady Slipper Orchid), potted and ready to bloom. This is the ideal orchid for amateurs, and distinguished for the lasting quality of its blossoms (in the pot, or on your shoulder).

The orchids you see in florist's shops—mauve, rose and lilac—are mostly *Cattleyas*. A *Cattleya* blooms all year (*Cypripedium* only in the winter). You can also get a *Cattleya* for $3, and wear it for weeks—if you're careful. A Christmas corsage of the same orchid costs from $5 to $7 and you can raise it in the kitchen, and save your beau the price.

A Boston lady wrote to *Horticulture* † last winter, to tell about an orchid she had for Christmas. She pinned it on her coat, and wore it to church. And

---

* From *L. Sherman Adams Co., Wellesley, Mass*—or your own florist.

† A magazine published by the Massachusetts Horticultural Society.

when she came home, she put it in water. She did
this for nine consecutive Sundays (*over two months!*)

> *. . . and on each Sunday the flower was much ad-*
> *mired for its beauty and freshness . . . On Sunday,*
> *February 23, the orchid was still sending forth its*
> *delightful fragrance, when a Doubting Thomas*
> *touched it, to see if it was real . . .*

She squeezed the stem, and touched the petals. It
was a *Cypripedium maudi* (white with green stripes)
—and its lovely petals turned to brown.

> *. . . The fragile flower had survived blizzards, and*
> *varying temperatures . . .*

And if that Doubting Thomas hadn't touched it, it
might be blooming yet.

Once, orchid-growing was confined to horticultur-
ists and millionaires. But not any more. Stenog-
raphers are raising blossoms in the bathroom. And
Captain Helge Ellesen grows them in his cabin on
the Kungsholm.

The needs of an orchid are simple. Plenty of air
and sunlight—but the sunlight should come through
a curtain, so that it won't be too strong. Enough
moisture, but not too much—or the roots will rot.
. . . And that is all there is to raising what many
people consider the most fragile flower in the world.

*   *   *

Next time you pass a potted geranium, buy it. Then you are started. If you are a budgeteer, allow yourself a quarter to two dollars a week for plants and flowers . . . and what if you *do* give up a few movies?

To learn about flowers, send for seed and plant catalogues, and write for information. Most nurseries will tell you anything you want to know. Go to the Flower Shows, and the Markets.

To begin with, get a few bulbs for house plants, and plant them in the fall, for Christmas blooms— hyacinths . . . narcissi . . . tulips and daffodils.

A woman cannot live by bread alone. And the Persians had a verse for a girl on a budget:

> *If thou of fortune be bereft*
> *And in thy store there be but left*
> *Two loaves, sell one, and with the dole*
> *Buy hyacinths to feed thy soul.*

Or buy some lily-of-the valley roots. Pot them in moss or sand, and water them well—and in three weeks, you'll have blossoms to nourish your soul.

There are bulbs called *Colchicums* that were made in heaven for cliff dwellers, and girls who live in one room. *Colchicums* bloom without soil or water, in heat or darkness. And the only way to discourage them is to keep them in cold storage. They look like little crocuses. And all they ask is to be let alone. Colchicums make dainty boutonnieres—and keep fresh without water for a week or ten days.

Irene Hayes says that girls should wear flowers, even if they have to pay for them. Miss Hayes, who has a flower shop on Park Avenue, practices what she preaches, and charges it up to advertising. Last time I saw her she had on a dark little hat, with orchids snuggling against pert white wings, and on her shoulder a pale cluster of *Laelias* (Vestal - Virgin orchids).

Most corsages (if not handled) will last a second day, when refrigerated over night. Raw stems should be put in water. And if the stems are wrapped, the flower should be placed in an airtight cellophane bag, which you can get from a florist, or in the five-and-ten.

Ice is the great reviver—ice and sometimes cold water. Give gardenias a thorough drenching on blossoms and leaves, and keep them in the refrigerator. And do the same for roses and carnations. But never sprinkle a camelia.

*   *   *

The best flower buys are tulips, in the spring—tulips have the longest life of any spring flower. And once they were the most expensive flower in the world. In 1636 a bulb called *Semper Augustus* was sold for 13,000 florins, two gray horses and a new carriage, four oxen, eight swine, a suit of clothes, a silver drinking cup, and a bed. A merchant gave his entire fortune for the bulb . . . and then it was eaten by a sailor who thought it was an onion.

Tulips were first cultivated by the Turks. Then the Dutch went mad about them—a madness known to history as *Tulipomania*. And for 300 years all the best bulbs came from Holland. But now we are doing very well with them in America.

Regal and rubrum lilies are good summer-time buys—and snapdragon, stock, bachelor buttons and daisies. (Once I had an African daisy corsage that lasted a fortnight). In the fall, gladioli, zinnias, asters and chrysanthemums stand up well. And anemones last for a week.

To make flowers last, stick them up to their necks in a pail of water, and keep them there three hours. Then keep them away from radiators, and out of drafts. Cut their stems every day and change the water . . . or if you are too lazy or busy, just fill the vases with fresh water—or add a few lumps of ice. Steam heat parches flowers. And sudden blasts of cold air take the life out of them. When you open windows at night, put your posies in the closet.

Most people buy a dozen of everything . . . a dozen roses, a dozen glads, or a dozen iris. A less expensive and more satisfying way is to buy *one of this, and three of that, four of these and two of*

those . . . or even just *one*—like the man who sent
Dorothy Parker *one perfect rose*. Only Mrs. Parker
didn't like it and cried aloud: `

> *Why is it no one ever sent me yet*
>   *One perfect limousine, do you suppose?*
> *Ah no, it is always just my luck to get*
>   *One perfect rose!* *

*   *   *   .

Someone said something lovely about our house
once. She said she had come to call half a dozen
times.

"But I never rang," she said, "because I could see
you were going to have a party."

"But we *weren't* going to have a party," we said.

·"Why, everything looked so beautiful! . . . the
rooms were filled with flowers," she said.

Mother collected likely vases, and flower holders
(needle frogs, that look like hair brushes). She
placed vases in front of mirrors for double effect.
And she knew how to eke out with huckleberry and
laurel, before it became a trick of the trade.

In the fall, when the foliage was brightest, we cut
red maple and boughs of crimson oak, and put them
in a mixture of glycerine and water (two of glycerine and one of water). And the flaming leaves not

---

* *Enough Rope.*

only stayed bright and glorious all winter, but took on a lovely lustre that glowed like the cheek of an apple. . . . We picked snowberries to mix with the roses—and Japanese barberries for the copper bowl that held marigolds.

In the spring, we gathered flowering quince and forsythia, and boughs of cherry and apple. We made criss-cross slits at the ends of the branches, and put them in glass urns that druggists used to have in their window. (Papa bought out a druggist once.)

An 18-inch clear vase for dogwood and other giant flowers is a good investment. Buying vases is a pleasant hobby—and few people have the right containers for different flowers. Clear glass is always lovely and usually recommended by decorators, whose second choice is often white china. White china is something I particularly dislike.

Colored bowls are inexpensive if you don't go looking for them, but just pick them up when you can. And if you have enough of them, there will be no danger of not having the right shade to contrast or harmonize with all the flowers that grow.

Chicken wire, bent into a rough ball, makes a good substitute for a needle frog. If you use it in a glass bowl, you can conceal it with crumpled cellophane, which looks charming in water.

*   *   *

The other day I heard a lecture by an eminent, and most cautious, horticulturist who said an amazing thing.

"It is doubtful," he said, "whether more than two colors can be successfully combined by the amateur." . . . The Garden Club ladies nodded their approval.

"Green and white," he continued, "may prevent discord. But the adjustment of three colors will always require the services of an expert." .. . . And the ladies acquiesced.

Well, all I can say is I wish they could condone a brazen attitude, and look upon the wild hues I have combined this day. I have purple gladioli, with white and orchid stock and deep-red snap dragons. That is on one chest. On the other I have rubrum and fragrant regal lilies, with azure delphinium, and lavender lupine. On the coffee table is a bowl of violet asters, and zinnias of crimson and strange reds and tawny pinks, hobnobbing audaciously with purple petunias.

I am afraid if the horticultural gentleman saw them he would have a headache—and the Garden Club ladies would fidget and wince. But it is fun to weave colors to make a rainbow blush . . . and a gaudy bouquet feeds my hungry soul.

Chapter Nine

If you can keep your head —

Here is a toast that I want to give
To a girl I'll never know;
To the girl who's going to take my place
When it's time for me to go!

Nice men are fussy about how girls drink, and most girls are not very good with alcohol.

A beautiful thing to remember would be that you will never feel better than you do on three drinks, from then on you never can tell . . . and there's always tomorrow.

You may not get silly or sloppy, but you are practically certain to look less attractive. The things you say will not be as clever or as funny as you think. And if you don't get cute, you may get shrill and shrewish.

Alcohol makes most people sloppy, or amorous, or quarrelsome—and sometimes its makes them all three. But usually it makes them happy first—which is why they take it. Alcohol removes inhibitions. It gives us self-confidence, and makes us brave—like that scared little mouse who got drunk and shook his whiskers and shouted:

"Now bring on that damn cat!"

It is all very well to become brave and happy. But the trouble is, that is only the beginning—and the rest is not so good.

Alcohol promotes maundering confidences, and countenances careless love-making. First you're tight, and then you're loose. And there's no consolation in a hangover.

The first drink or two will probably brighten you up—make your eyes sparkle, and your cheeks flush. The third may make you too darn sure of yourself. Then the flush is less becoming, and usually goes to the wrong places—to your throat, or—God help us—to your nose.

The older you are, the less liquor suits you. It has launched many a maiden, coy but undeterred, on a predatory quest that has made her want to die of her mortification in the morning.

When you get where you begin to wilt at 5 P.M., the deteriorating effect of alcohol is in proportion to its exhilaration. And it is always the same old story. When you work up to a certain emotional pitch (on three drinks say, before dinner), you want another, to postpone the depressing fall of spirits—and that's the time to stop. . . . Then be smart, sweet maid, and let who will get tight. Order dinner on the second drink. When you entertain, remember it's the drinks before you eat that make all the trouble, and quickies are deadly.

> *She lolled at a cocktail bar*
> *At five in the afternoon,*
> *Outside was the glory of sunset—*
> *In the offing, a slim new moon.*
> *She lounged at the cocktail bar*
> *While the night with stars was rife,*
> *She drank in the clatter, the piffle, the din—*
> *O boy, was she seeing life! ***

If you can keep your head when all about you are losing theirs, you'll be glad. And here are a few things to remember:

When it's a long time between drinks, you can drink more—but there are no prizes for it. And drinking the boys under the table is old hat. The safest of all drinks is whiskey and soda, or whiskey and plain water. Whiskey is usually the best thing

* Jazbo of Old Dubuque, in the *Chicago Tribune.*

to drink before eating, and always the best afterward.

Liqueurs are sweet and apt to be sickish. And you should never toss them off (as some girls do), or drink a toast with them. A liqueur is served only after dinner, in a tiny (one ounce) glass. And you should sip it like a lady.

The reason that Brandy, taken as a ·liqueur, is sometimes served in a very large balloon glass (called a *snifter* or *inhaler*) is because epicures like to cradle the glass in their hands, thereby warming the liquor and creating an aroma. This is a trick of connoisseurs with fine old Brandy, and only show-offs sniff pretentiously at every-day stuff.

A *Side Car,* the King of all Cocktails, is made with two parts Brandy, one of Triple Sec, and one of lime juice. (*Parts* means you measure with anything you want—jiggers or water glasses—depending upon how many you are mixing for.) Just keep your proportions straight . . . and remember tomorrow!

Brandy is drunk with charged water, making a Brandy and soda, or Brandy highball. Brandy and soda is too much for most people, but in the old days no gentleman would drink any liquor that did not come from the grape, and it had to be either brandy or wine. Whiskey and Gin were good enough for cabmen and stevedores, but that was all—until, in the 70's and 80's, there was a time when no good brandy was to be had—something about a vine disease and a grape pest—a nasty little louse—that ravaged French vineyards. Then the thirsty gentlemen had to drink liquors distilled from grain, and also—because Clarets and Burgundies were no longer fine—they turned to Champagne.

Champagnes in those days were on the sweet side, and considered *le vin des cocottes*. . . . Queen Victoria, by the way, doted on Claret, and tried to woo Albert from his lovely Hock. Champagne she considered immoral.

Champagne is happy and exciting—but mix nothing with it. . . . And look out for sweet drinks. Sickening, saccharine potions will make you ill before they make you happy.

Cocktails, heavy with tinned fruit juices and grenadine, were intended to camouflage bathtub gin, and anyone who mixes them is guilty of misdemeanor and sin, and no one should go to her parties. Girls have become pariahs for adding a dash of maple syrup to a whiskey sour. But they were the little women who splashed marshmallow and whipped cream on salads . . . so nobody cares.

Cocktails are usually drunk before luncheon or dinner, when tomato juice would be better for you. Cocktails are an American invention. And should be served, I think, as the French serve *apéritifs*—as a pick-me-up in the afternoon, when you've nothing better to do. It is ghastly to drink them after meals, and a mistake to touch them till the day's work's done.

Apéritif means appetite-opener. A Frenchman has his *apéritif* an hour before dinner, to give his appetite a chance to grow—and he does not take so much as a peanut with it.

Canapés and hors d'oeuvres, as served with cocktails, are a meal in themselves, and will spoil a good dinner any night.

To make an end of cocktails, you can serve a dry Sherry or dry Vermouth, either straight or with bitters. California sherries are blessedly cheap, considerably less bother than cocktails, and quite fashionable. If you serve Sherry as an appetizer, you can go on serving it through the meal, but you must be sure it is not too sweet.

"Wine," as Benjamin Franklin once remarked, "is a constant proof that God loves us, and loves to see us happy."

American wine growers, co-operating tardily with the Almighty, are doing their best to make wine a national drink, and there is no reason why they should not succeed.

Wine—in moderation—is good for you. It is better than beer (not so fattening)—and it is *so cheap!* White wines should be chilled before serving, and not served until after the soup. Red wines

—excepting Burgundies—should be served at room temperature. Still Burgundy should be slightly chilled, and sparkling Burgundy should be iced.

American Champagnes are looking up, and for a very special two-some you might be proud to serve a dry California. It will set you back about $3, and you should have a quart, because a pint is not enough to give two people a glow.

To make *Champagne Cocktails,* drop half a cube of sugar in a cocktail glass, squirt the sugar with a dash of bitters, put in an ice cube, and fill with Champagne. Then squeeze a bit of lemon peel over the top, to coax out the oil, and drop the peel (a twist no bigger than your finger nail) into the glass.

It is rather important, I think, to have the proper glasses, and to serve your liquor with a touch of elegance. You can buy acceptable glasses in the ten-cent store . . . but keep away from the colored ones. Colored wine glasses were contrived long ago to conceal the cloudiness of poor wines, and are not quite smart. Four of each kind are enough for a girl whose parties are smallish, but it is provident to have a number of spares for highballs.

You should have Sherry glasses, in which you can also serve Vermouth and Port. Port, the English aristocrat's wine of wines, is a dessert wine, served with crackers and cheese.

Your cocktail glasses will do for Champagne, if

they are clear and colorless—or you can use your wine glasses for cocktails.

A Collins glass is higher than a highball glass, but unless you go for juleps and punches, and long drinks generally, you can just stick with the high-ball glasses.*

If you serve Old Fashioneds, you must also have Old Fashioned glasses.

Gin drinks do not taste so good in silver or pewter. A Martini is stronger than Scotch—and if the gin is not good, it will make you sicker quicker. A Martini should never be shaken, but poured over ice into a pitcher, and gently stirred. Millions of Martinis are ruined every year by professional and amateur mixers—and do you know how? *They don't wash the olives!*

The best cocktail shaker is simple and good-looking, and made of clear glass, the kind you can buy in a drug store for about 98 cents. And the finest

___

* A highball glass holds 8 ounces, which is one cup. A Tom Collins holds 12 ounces. And an outsize Tom Collins holds 16 ounces, which is one pint.

cocktail glasses are never dolled up with foolishness, such as the Stars and Stripes, and mermaids—or the Katzenjammer Kids.

*   *   *

I have been wondering whether to give you recipes, or let you look them up somewhere else. And I have decided that it will be convenient to have recipes for drinks and food in the same little book. There are no Pink Ladies in the list, nor Angels' Kisses—only seven standard drinks, and one I made up myself. And that would be funny, if it were not so good, because I think women who make up drinks are nuts.

The trouble is women are so ingenious—a dash of cranberry, and a little canned pear juice . . . but it's all a mistake, girls. Save Aunt Hatty's strawberry jam for the toast, and stick with the barmen.

Over 3,000 cocktails have been invented since repeal, but less than fifty are worth the mixing.

For a complete and sophisticated little bar you will need seven essential liquors, and your initial investment will be about $12.50. You could do it cheaper than this, but it is best to buy standard brands, because you don't want to make people sick, do you? Or have them say, "Oh, she's the one with the bathtub gin"—or "that terrible rum"?

You should have a bottle each of Sherry, Gin,

Scotch, Rye or Bourbon, Vermouth, Rum, and Angostura Bitters. (Bitters cost 75 cents, and last forever.)

Sherry is for mild and stylish drinkers; Gin for Martinis and Tom Collins; Scotch is for Highballs; Rye or Bourbon for Old Fashioneds (Bourbon is smoother, I think); Rum is for Daiquiris—and Bacardi for Bacardis.

Bacardi is the family name of the distillers of a very special Cuban rum that is not really rum at all —but *brandy!* Only everyone calls it rum. Bartenders used to make alleged Bacardis out of Puerto Rican and Virgin Island rums. But the family jumped on them, and now the Supreme Court says it is illegal to use anything except Bacardi in a Bacardi cocktail.

All drinks should be measured with an ounce-and-a-half jigger—and if you skimp, they will be wishy-washy.

Highballs: a jigger of Scotch with ice and charged or plain water. Or a jigger of Rye with ice and ginger ale, or charged water.

Martinis: two parts gin to one of Vermouth. Almost
everybody prefers a dry Vermouth. Stir (not shake)
until really cold, and serve with an olive in each glass.
Martinis can be made in a pitcher, kept in the refrigerator, and poured in the kitchen.

A luke-warm cocktail getting warmer is about as
appetizing as a fried egg bleeding to death in a
pool of bacon fat.

The original *Old Fashioned* had no nonsense
about it—nothing but a jigger of liquor and a dash
of Angostura. But now an Old Fashioned must
have a stick of pineapple, a maraschino cherry, and
a slice each of orange and lemon. O tempora, O
mores, O girls . . . it's all your doing!

Old Fashioneds: Place a lump of sugar in each glass—a
dash of bitters and a teaspoon or so of water—and then
crush the sugar. Add a cube of ice, pour over the ice
a jigger of Bourbon or Rye—and add the fruit. *Old
Fashioneds* can be made with Scotch or Rum—and
then they are *Scotch Old Fashioneds,* or *Rum Old
Fashioneds.*

Manhattans: Two jiggers of Bourbon or Rye to one of
Vermouth, and a dash of Angostura. Add ice and stir
(never shake), and serve with a cherry in each glass.
You can use either a red or green cherry, but the syrupy
sweetness of a maraschino makes the drink a bit more
velvety, I think.

Bacardis: The juice of half a large lime, half a teaspoon
of granulated sugar, one and a half jiggers of white
Barcardi. Shake well with ice. . . .

This formula was given me by my friend Senor Rafael Valiente, who is host at the famous Bacardi Bar in Havana, and is the only proper recipe in a world flooded with funny, phony ones.

I forgot to say that if your Billy or Tommy likes Daiquiris, you must get a bottle of Grenadine (55 cents, and a lot for your money). Grenadine—a maraschino syrup—is used in many of the flossier drinks, and is on the saccharine or sickening side.

Daiquiris: The juice of half a lime, a fourth of a jigger of Grenadine, and a jigger of rum.

People in bar rooms do a lot of arguing about *Bacardis* and *Daiquiris* and hardly anybody knows what he's talking about. It all goes back to Mark Hanna, an American statesman who went to Cuba for a vacation, and made up a drink with Bacardi and limes that he called a Daiquiri. Mr. Hanna didn't put any Grenadine in it—it was exactly the same as the Bacardi recipe I just gave you. And in a little while, it became the most popular cocktail in the world. But, by and by, along came Prohibition . . . and there was no Bacardi to be had. Then, to kill the taste of bad rum, speakeasies started using Grenadine instead of sugar . . . and that is how Daiquiris came to have Grenadine in them.

When limes are green and juicy, they are better in all drinks than lemons . . . but bottled lime juice is a horrid thing. And a *Tom Collins* mix is flat, sweet and pallid . . . when compared with a *proper* Collins.

Tom Collins: Squeeze into a tall glass a whole lime or lemon, stir in a heaping teaspoon of powdered sugar, and add a jigger and a half of gin. Then add ice, fill the glass with charged water, and stir again, up from the bottom.

*   *   *

If all be true that I do think
There are five reasons we should drink:
Good wine—a friend—or being dry—
Or lest we should be, by and by—
Or any other reason why.*

One winter I lived in Haiti, up in the hills of Petionville. And in my garden there was a pool twenty feet long, with little lime trees on one side, and a big granadilla on the other. A granadilla bears golden fruit, as big and beautiful as a child's balloon. Another name for it is passion fruit, but that nasty red stuff you get in drug stores is not passion fruit at all. The juice of the true fruit is fragrant, and yellow, and thick as the filling of a lemon pie. And you can get it in pint bottles for about a dollar.

One day Sylvio Cator, who was world champion

* *Causae Bibendi*—17th Century.

broad jumper, came to call, and I was boasting about how long my pool was.

"Pooh," said Sylvio, "that's nothing. I could jump over your old pool with my eyes shut."

"Bet," I said, because how did I know he was a broad jumper.

Sylvio hopped, skipped and jumped—he jumped the whole 20 feet! . . . And that called for a drink.

We began with Haitian rum, and added green lime juice. We sweetened it with honey, and then we squeezed a granadilla, and we mixed them all together—two of rum, and one of lime—half of honey, and half of granadilla. And when we tasted it, we thought it was about the best drink we ever had—so Sylvio named it the *Eleanor Early*.

*   *   *

When I lived in Dominica, I had a little lad named Happy Boy who climbed tall palms like a monkey, to shake down fruit filled with coconut milk, that Auxanges mixed with Gin to make a long cold drink. And if it had not been so good, it would have been better. Because I was trying to write a book . . . and what I wrote on a coconut-gin never counted.

In Dominica, sour oranges grew gold in the sun, and 10,000 little trees were hung with limes like baubles on Christmas trees. The best rum punches are made with sour oranges and the juice of green limes. There was a man in Roseau who made the punch for Queen Victoria's Jubilee, and he told me that the reason his punches were so good was that he put a tiny pinch of salt in them.

West Indian islands are lovely places to drink, because rum is a shilling a quart, and when you are out of doors all the time, it hardly ever goes to your head. And losing your head is pretty dumb, because you don't have to lose your head to have a good time.

* * *

There is one kind of man that is never good for a girl. And that is the beautiful bum who cannot drink. He comes in several guises, but usually runs to a pattern. The dipsomaniac is almost always pitiful (*he needs me so!*). Inevitably weak (*poor darling—he tries so hard*). And, in the earlier stages, personable. He is ingratiating, confiding, and sometimes charming. And he hasn't an ounce of what your grandmother called *character*.

The boy who "can't hold his liquor" may—if he is young enough—learn how. But if he has been holding it badly for a long time, no one can teach him—and the girl who tries is ordering despair in double doses. If your hero is a heel, get smart, get tough—*get out!*

When you were in school, you read *Les Miserables* —and probably you read this, only you weren't old enough to think about it:

Upon the first goblet he read this inscription: Monkey Wine; upon the second: Lion Wine; upon the third: Sheep Wine; upon the fourth: Swine Wine. These four inscriptions expressed the four descending degrees of drunkenness: the first, that which enlivens; the second, that which irritates; the third, that which stupifies; finally the last, that which brutalizes.

Translated in terms of your own experience—too much liquor makes a man gay—and that's a nice beginning. But then he gets nasty, and that's horrid. Then he gets stupid—and that is worse. . . . Then he gets ideas.

"When de Debil cain't go," said Auxanges, "he send de Rum."

There are times to forgive and times to forget a man, and it is easier to leave some of them alone than try to reform them.

*   *   *

I didn't mean to go into this drinking business, like Carrie Chapman Catt with the W.C.T.U. at her heels, but now that we are this far I am going to tell you a Celestial principle.

The Chinese have a word called *Chih* that means a *consciousness of shame,* also *moral pride,* together meaning that we should be ashamed to do anything contrary to our sense of moral pride. *Chih* would be a nice motto for a girl. . . . And in case she forgot it—here is another: *Never Explain—Never Regret* . . . Regret is an awful waste of energy. You can't build on it, and it is only good for wallowing in. . . . So saying—we will get on to Canapés.

Chapter Ten

Some girls Know How —

A canapé is little cousin to an hors d'oeuvre, and you need never serve more than two of a kind —unless you want to show off. Sometimes it is fun to show off, but it is simpler to take things easy, and I am going to give you a few little items that you can run up with one hand, while you are squeezing limes with the other.

The distinction between an hors d'oeuvre and a canapé is a fork and your fingers. Sometimes hors d'oeuvres are a first course at a formal dinner, and served at the table—and in French and Italian restaurants they almost always precede the *table d'hote*.

Sometimes they are served at bridge parties, after-noon teas, and after-theatre supper parties. They may be arranged on an individual plate for each person, or on a tray or platter, and passed so that each guest may help himself. If you are serving hors d'oeuvres at dinner, have a small plate to park them on placed on the service plate before your guests sit down (here I am going on like Emily Post).

Canapés are something that look well in the hand, as salesgirls say of a frock. They should neither be so large nor so elaborate as to explode in the fingers, but a tidy tidbit to pop in the mouth.

The etiquette of serving them is simple as ABC. First you pass the tray with the cocktails, then you pass the one with the appetizers. Then you put what's left on the table, and let people help themselves.

If you are serving dinner afterward, don't press liquor on your guests, or ply them with canapés. If you are not, heap the tray with tid-bits, and do as the Bible says.*

If you are terribly lazy and don't care much about doing things nicely, you can buy ready-made canapé spreads, a package of popcorn, and some potato chips. But if you want to be a clever hostess, you will get some gadgets to cut the bread. Get rounds and squares, and half moons, maybe . . . and small

* *Take thine ease, eat, drink, and be merry.* Luke XII. 19.

ones, because, being thrifty, you can make your spreads go further—and get two canapés out of each slice of bread. . . . But whatever you do, *don't* get cheap pastes in ten-cent tubes, because the stuff that is in them is about as seductive as ringside sawdust. There was a tinned lobster paté I had at a party two years ago that makes me sick even to think about. . . .

Raw *finocchi* (Italian celery) makes a good appetizer—if you can get it. And little raw baby carrots—scrubbed and scraped—are nice to nibble. Keep them in the hydrator in the refrigerator, or in cold water, so that they won't get limp and spongy before they're eaten.

Set out your cocktail things before you dress, with the appetizers that won't spoil with waiting. Dinner should be late, to allow plenty of time for perfecting touches. And don't rush through drinks, because rushing spoils everything.

* * *

Lest you think I meant to condemn all patés when I blasted that long-ago lobster, I want to tell you about one that is particularly good. It is made from the turkeys that are raised and smoked on that famous farm in Pinesbridge. A whole turkey is awfully expensive, but minced meat is not, and—personally—I'd rather have a few jars of paté on the shelf, than a big bird in the refrigerator. A recipe book comes with each jar, that tells how to make epicurean dishes for brunch and supper, and paté puffs for cocktails.

*　　*　　*

Cocktails and canapés—just for two—will make a man think how nice it would be to have you around all the time. And the girl who can't wangle a proposal with a cocktail shaker and a chafing dish is too dumb to deserve a husband. . . . I have warned you not to have the drinks too sweet—and I'd suggest that you just don't bother with peanut butter canapés, or stuffed prunes (some women serve the *damndest* things). Don't give him onions, unless you know he likes them . . . and go easy on chives.

If he is taking you to the theatre, don't try to have dinner first—but just a bite and a couple of drinks. Don't stuff him with popcorn, olives and salted nuts, if you want him to be nice to you. And don't expect a man with a lot on his mind to make love when he's worried. Just pour another drink, pass the canapés—and don't worry. Don't ask him What's the matter? And don't say, Darling, don't you love me any more?

After the theatre, go back to your apartment for supper (see next chapter). And if the play was a flop and he didn't enjoy himself very much, don't be especially affectionate. Cuddling up in a taxi may bring him around, but you might as well wait.

*   *   *

A girl can do a lot of things with bacon, if she wants to bother. But bacon burns quickly and gets smelly, so that it is not the daintiest thing to fool with. You can cut cheese into one-inch blocks, roll a strip of bacon around each square, and secure it with a toothpick. Or—instead of cheese—have chunks of lobster meat—or big, pitted olives. Fry or broil quickly, turning so that the bacon will cook evenly. Drain on brown paper, and serve hot on toothpicks.

A girl can make all sorts of cracker spreads with tinned fish, or chicken, or Smithfield ham—and a little ingenuity. Here is one for a starter—and you can improvise some more. Crush boneless, skinless sardines with a biggish pinch of mustard, a dash of lemon juice, a few chopped pickles and a bit of minced onion. Moisten with mayonnaise.

Worcestershire is a help in home-made spreads. Finely chopped celery and green peppers are often good. And cheese blends with almost everything. Season rather highly, set in refrigerator to firm. And let people spread their own.

Joseph Hergesheimer told in one of his books about an hors d'oeuvre that has become very popular.

Some people make it with chipped beef that comes in jars, which is too dry—and untidy besides. Have the delicatessen slice the beef paper thin (the chipped kind comes in lopsided bits), and spread with cream cheese, moistened with a little cream. Then roll up like cigarettes, and chill.

Canned brown bread, sliced a quarter of an inch thick and browned in butter, makes a hearty foundation for a cheese spread. And here is a good spread:

Cheese Spread

1 package cream cheese	1 teaspoon Worcestershire
1 teaspoon anchovy paste	1 teaspoon mayonnaise

Mix together, and keep in refrigerator.

Most spreads are improved by a bit of finely minced onion.

Did you ever hear about the chef who cooked for Louis XIV, and committed suicide, because he forgot the fish course? Cooks take things hard. Once I stuffed and forgot a bunch of celery, and found it in the hydrator next morning. But I didn't commit suicide. I scraped out the cheese and made some canapés—and made soup with the celery.

I have two pet canapés, and this is one of them:

Cheese and Mushroom Canapés

1 package cream cheese	1 teaspoon minced onion
¼ pound mushrooms	Salt and pepper
Cream to moisten	

Slice the mushrooms in tiny pieces and cook for a few minutes in melted butter. Mix with onion, cheese and seasoning, and add cream to moisten.

Toast rounds of bread on one side, and butter the other. Spread buttered side with the mixture, and slide under the broiler, to puff and brown very slightly.

*   *   *

There used to be a restaurant in Copenhagen celebrated for its Smörgasbord, where they served *pyramid portions* of shrimps. A man named Oskar owned the place, and among Oskar's famed patrons were the Duke and Duchess of Windsor, who used to fly to Denmark just to eat shrimps. They were such good press agents that before long Oskar employed twenty-five girls to do nothing but just shuck shrimps all day.

Oskar made a sandwich called *Shrimps in a Crowd* that he sent by air to shrimp addicts all over the world. His menu was 45 inches long—with the front side devoted to delicatessen, and the back to drinks. And every portion was so generous, that people who ate regularly at Oskar's became simply enormous. The menu said there were 20 to 45 shrimps in a *Pyramid Portion,* and 130 to 140 in *Shrimps in a Crowd.*

Oskar told me that he thought—next to women, American men liked shrimps better than anything in the world. Which was just being funny. But men *do* like shrimps. And if you serve them icy cold, with a toothpick in each—and a bowl of Thousand Island Dressing to dunk them in—you'll see. (There is a recipe for the dressing, in the next chapter.)

Liverwurst Appetizers make a hearty snack. Skin half a pound of the best liverwurst, and mash it up with a quarter of a pound of sweet butter. Don't use any salt, but shake in plenty of freshly ground black pepper. (You must get yourself a little grinder.) Cream well, and keep overnight in the refrigerator. Spread between thin slices of French rolls, and toast on both sides. Serve hot.

For a quickie, smear bread very thinly with prepared mustard, sprinkle with grated Cheddar cheese, sprinkle with paprika, and pop under the broiler until the cheese melts. . . . If you don't like mustard, use just cheese.

Two packages of cream cheese, mixed with an egg and half a teaspoon of grated onion make a spread that puffs as it browns, and is quite tasty.

Lean bacon can be cut in squares, with scissors, and broiled on a square of bread, sprinkled with Parmesan, or spread with Cheddar.

You can make cream cheese balls with butter paddles, roll them in ground nut meats, and put them in the refrigerator to firm. Or make them awfully small, and put them between a couple of salted pecans. Blend snappy cheese with sherry, and make it into little balls, and roll in nut meats. Take the skin off thinly sliced salami, and roll a slice tightly around a small gherkin, or a big stuffed olive. . . . And here is the canapé that is my second pet:

Bacon and Cheese Canapés

1 tablespoon butter	¼ teaspoon mustard
6 tablespoons snappy or Cheddar cheese	¼ teaspoon paprika
	Salt and pepper
4 slices bacon, cooked and chopped	1 unbeaten egg

Mix well together, spread on the unbuttered side of toast rounds, and brown under the broiler . . . and you needn't be particular about amount of cheese.

Now that I have given you my cocktail standbys, we will proceed to sterner fare—to *brunch,* and dinner, and suppers, plain and fancy.

Chapter Eleven

Baby, How Do You Do It!

This chapter is going to be written right out of my heart, because I am as emotional about food as moonlight—and the scarlet of a newburg can shake me like a cry of bugles going by.

It is written for the benefit of girls, who, like myself, not only love to eat, but love to entertain—and for every girl who loves a man, and wants to make him happy.

* * *

Experience with cooking articles published in some magazines and newspapers has led me to believe that certain alleged cooks never cook the things they write about. That is why every recipe here is Tested, Tried, and True. On some I have built a local renown . . . all are a part of my regular repertoire. And if I am not old and famous, neither am I young and innocent—and my culinary life began at eight.

Maybe you are not much of a home-body. Maybe you don't know farina from forcemeat, or romaine from a ramekin. You are a debutante, perhaps—or a stenographer on $22 a week—or a career woman with a lot on your mind. But you can turn to, if you want, and be the girl who's the wonderful cook, and gives the swell parties.

All you have to do is concentrate on simple foods—don't dehydrate the steak—or make salads that look like valentines. Stick with one-dish meals, patronize casseroles and double-boilers. And, if you plan ahead—keep things from burning—don't get flour on your nose—or make the drinks too sweet, you'll have the boys crying, *"Baby, how do you do it!"*

You may be a natural-born hausfrau, though you never guessed it—and a little practice, maybe, will bring out the epicure in you. Anyhow, I'll give you some recipes, and you can find out—recipes to make a reputation on. And a little advice on the side.

When you give a party, have lots of flowers—mix the drinks with care—go easy on the appetizers. Have the hot food hot—the cold food cold—and plenty of both. Light the candles—put on some more lipstick—and have a good time.

*   *   *

I am a woman who can take an old hen, and give you Chicken à la King, to melt in your mouth . . . or a cheap cut of beef and—with a little red wine— make a stew to remember. I have a curry that any green girl can make—a fool-proof rabbit—a $2500 soufflé—and a grand pandowdy. Soups are one of my specialties—and lobster my *pièce de résistance*.

Knowing how to cook is a pleasant way of getting what you want, because a well fed man—like any other well fed animal—is so good-natured a child can handle him. Most men have a frank and sensuous appreciation of good food—and, since nothing is sweeter to a woman than admiration—gratifying the boys is a lovely circle. First we make them happy. Then they make us glad.

Woman's place is still, I believe, in the vicinity of the kitchen—only now it's the kitchenette, and more fun.

In England it is considered not quite nice to speak of the food, but in France a guest sends his compliments to the chef. And that is right. Nobody is adult enough to get along without approval— and flattery is almost as good for a girl as love.

In one of Balzac's stories, he tells of a girl at whom nobody ever looked twice, who needed only kisses and love letters to change her into a beauty. Well, flattery isn't the panacea that love is, but it's a big help. And one way of getting it is as simple as this: Give a man a comfortable chair to sit in, a good drink to drink, and good food to eat—and, my dear, he'll be around all the time, just flattering the life out of you!

*   *   *

Cooking for my own gratification and a man's lusty pleasure is my quaint idea of a beautiful time . . . but sometimes I think of Grandma, and wonder how she liked it.

Grandpa had a penchant for boiled dinners that smelled up the house, and sometimes the neighborhood. Corned beef and cabbage, cooked in the pot with potatoes and carrots, parsnips and turnips— served with mustard pickle and cold slaw . . . with hot bread . . . and apple and mince pies, and marble cake and preserved pears. Grandpa always had three desserts—and Grandma did what was known as "drudge all day over a hot stove," and "wear her fingers to the bone." While Grandpa, with unrepentant pleasure, ate himself into high blood pressure.

Many of us are better cooks than our grandmothers, and achieve triumphs that would have kept the old ladies in the kitchen from sun-up. Men in Grandma's day brought home the bacon, but they never cooked it—and Grandma and her league worked over-time.

When a girl rolls up her sleeves, she likes a little co-operation. Men who can cook are nice men to have around. They bring you funny gifts in paper bags—little black peppers and a grinder, jars of smoked turkey paté, green chives growing in a basket, Bahamian mustard . . . and there are some lovely souls who bring liquor.

A society of Gourmets in New York had a poll to determine the foods men prefer, and the results went like this:

> Steaks and Roasts
> Chicken, Ham and Eggs
> Stews, Hash, and Baked Beans
> Corned Beef and Cabbage

The boys voted for meals that *stick to the ribs*—heavy soups and hot breads—apple pie and ice cream, pandowdy, and puddings.

If this were a book for Brides, I should stick out

my chest at this point and talk about Pot Roasts and
Swiss Steaks, and what a smart girl can do with
Bottom of the Round. But unless you are a little
woman with time on your hands, you are not interested in the dredge-sear-and-baste school. Easily
prepared foods are more down your street—inexpensive but not too commonplace—with a *stick-to-
the-ribs* wallop—and something dandy for dessert.

There is a legend that American men do not like
sauces—but they always reach for the ketchup, or
page A-1 and a bottle of Worcestershire. The truth
is men are tired of dull, unseasoned foods, and the
girl who gets a reputation for sauces has a feather
in her cap.

To be a good cook, you've got to be adventurous—
take a chance—and try a few innovations. A girl
should have her *specialties,* or made-up dishes. She
should be able to concoct her own Spaghetti, her
distinctive Curry, and special Hamburgers.

She should have a special shelf for herbs and spices.
I have a little red box with eleven packets of herbs
in it that cost a dollar, and a basket with twelve jars
of spices.* And I use them all the time, with their
little charts that tell me how much to use, and in
what. Without my Spice Shelf, I'd feel like a
plumber who left his tools at the shop.

In my Condiment Cabinet are three wines—Sau-

* From *Bellows Gourmet Bazaar,* 67 East 52 St., New York.

terne, Sherry and Burgundy. I have also Worcester-shire Sauce, A-1, and Tabasco (go easy on Tabasco!). Curry, prepared Mustards and Ketchup, and a bottle of Mango Chutney (which some people dislike).

To facilitate using left-overs, I have Macaroni, Noodles, Rice, Tomato Paste, a tin of Salted Nuts, and a package of coarse Bread Crumbs. And I keep on hand an assortment of canned soups and cheese.

This outlay ties up about ten dollars—and is cheap at the price. Once I interviewed a Viennese cook who told me that an extravagant amount of butter —judiciously used—makes all the difference between superior and inferior cooking. I agree on the butter, and feel the same way about condiments. This does not mean that I think you should bother with elaborate and fussy foods. And to prove it, I shall give recipes on the simple side. When you get proficient, you will want to experiment for yourself—and by that time, you won't need any suggestions from me.

First I am going to give you Onion Soup, which will do more to make a man loving than a full moon and honeysuckle (provided, of course, he likes onions). Ladle the soup from its covered casserole into biggish bowls of peasant pottery. Serve with French bread and a green salad. And waste no time on fripperies, for an onion soup needs no trimmings.

Onion Soup Au Gratin

4 biggish onions	1 quart of flavorful stock
4 tablespoons butter	. . . the easiest way to
4 tablespoons grated Par-	manage this is to get tins
mesan cheese	of beef consommé and
4 slices of toast	chicken bouillon, add a
1 cup dry wine, white or	can of strained lamb
red (optional)	broth, and toss in a few
Seasoning	bouillon cubes.

Peel and slice the onions and sauté slowly in butter in a covered saucepan for ten minutes, or until they are something more than golden. Stir frequently, and be sure that they do not get black. (Black onions are what make some people burp.) *Sauté* means *sizzle* very, very gently. An iron spider is a good thing to sauté in. Add stock, season to taste—a dash of celery salt and a pinch of thyme is good. After you have seasoned the stock, let it simmer with the onions for 15 or 20 minutes—then add wine. Pour into a big casserole, and float the toast on the top. Sprinkle with the grated cheese, and place in the oven (uncovered) until the cheese is browned.

Serve with a bowl of additional grated cheese, and thick slices of French bread, toasted but not buttered. Have plenty of ice-cold sweet butter on the table.

If you don't add wine, it will be just as good— only a little different. . . . And if you don't want to bother with dessert, you could have just fruit. Plain food and plenty of it is better than a mediocre

banquet—and a good soup and a dish of fruit is
nothing to be ashamed of.

Oyster Stew is good for a midnight snack, and
can be made in no time.

Oyster Stew
(for two)

12 oysters

The heart of celery, plus 3 or 4 tender white stalks.	1 jar of light cream
	1 kernel of garlic
	4 tablespoons of sweet butter
1 cup of milk	
1 level tablespoon flour	salt, pepper, and paprika.

Cut the celery very fine, and boil it gently with the
garlic in a scant cup of water for about 10 minutes.
Place flour and seasoning in a jar with the milk, and
shake until completely blended. Then cook in a double
boiler until creamy. Add celery with the water in
which it cooked—but fish out the garlic, and throw it
away. Melt two tablespoons of butter and add the
oysters with their juice. Heat gently until they get
plump, and curl at the edges—it takes only a few minutes. Add to double boiler. Heat the cream until it
shivers on top—be sure you don't scald it! Then pour
everything together into a tureen, and sprinkle with
lots of paprika. Add remaining butter.

Oyster crackers are silly little things, and thick
slices of buttered toast go better with stew. . . . To
keep milk or cream from sticking to a saucepan,
rinse the pan out in cold water, and don't dry it.

*   *   *

It is wonderful what a girl can do with canned soups . . . Black Bean, for example. Add (when heated) a few spoonfuls of sherry, float a thin slice of lime in each bowl, and sprinkle with paprika— and maybe the grated yolk of a hard-boiled egg.

Heat vegetable soups with a clove and a bay leaf or a bit of curry. Consult your spice and herb charts—add a dash of this and soupçon of that. Throw the tin in the ash barrel, hide the can opener —and tell him you made it.

Sherry is the best wine for soups, but it should be dry enough to curl your hair. Sherry will improve any meat stock, or glorify a bisque—and turtle soup without it is wretched.

To make a superior *Mushroom Soup,* slice thin and sauté a quarter of a pound of mushrooms in a couple of tablespoons of butter. Add a tin of mushroom soup, a jar of light cream, and a jigger of sherry, and sprinkle with paprika. . . . Many recipes say to discard mushroom stems and peel the caps, but I never do either, and my mushroom dishes are as good as anybody's (although a little darker).

Croutons

Trim the crusts from thickish slices of bread, spread liberally with butter (butter both sides), cut in inch cubes, place in a pan, and toast under very slow burner, shaking the pan back and forth to prevent burning, and to brown the bread evenly.

Another good thing to serve with soups (or with cheese, or for canapés) is Common Crackers, split, buttered and toasted. But I have been told it is difficult to buy them anywhere but in New England. In Boston we wed them with chowders, and couldn't get along without them.

*   *   *

Now I am going to talk about salads and then that Sunday morning brunch you're going to have for the boy friend. *Brunch* is a terrible word, but it seems to have passed into the language, for I found it just now in the dictionary.

Salads are supposed to be awfully smart. Personally, I consider them over-rated, being a woman who likes something I can get my teeth into. I knew a man who used to take me to the Ritz and embarrass me to death calling for holy oils and spices, and throwing leaves around like a juggler. Maybe the act gave me a complex. But, because I have a nice mahogany salad bowl, I use it once in a while. And when I do, I like to toss up something tasty.

The best salad bowls are made of wood. You can get an old-fashioned chopping bowl for about fifty cents—and never use soap to clean it, but just wipe it out with a paper towel.

The lettuce should be washed first, and dried, leaf

by leaf, in a clean towel. Then it should be tossed in the dressing, without bruising, until both sides of every leaf shine like seaweed in the sun.

A mixed green salad usually has, besides the lettuce, some watercress, slivered radishes, a little diced celery, or raw carrots, cucumbers, and perhaps a bit of shredded cabbage. The Chef's salad at the Boston Statler is seasoned with powdered tarragon and chervil (right in your little herb chest), and features sardines and slivers of cheese, and is considered pretty superior.

Almost everyone has her own version of French Dressing. Most people, I think, take one of vinegar to two of oil—but I take half and half. And this may be heresy—but I prefer the vinegar from a bottle of sweet pickles, and next to that I like red wine vinegar—the kind they use in cheap Italian restaurants.

I asked a man who boasts about his French Dressing how he makes it, and he said that he puts 8 tablespoons of olive oil and 4 of tarragon vinegar (or lime juice) in a cream jar, with a kernel or two of garlic (he scores the garlic to let the juice out), a heaping teaspoon of brown sugar, a little dry mustard, and plenty of salt and pepper—and shakes like mad.

Here is a dressing I made up myself that is better than most boughten ones. I make it for shrimps when I serve them as canapés, and keep it in the refrigerator between parties.

Thousand Island Dressing

½ cup chili sauce (get the best brand you can, because some of the cut-price ones are fearfully flat)

½ pint good mayonnaise

Juice of half a lime

1 tablespoon oyster cocktail sauce, or any hot tomato ketchup

2 tablespoons minced pimento

3 or 4 small minced pickles

½ small green pepper, minced

1 kernel garlic minced *very fine*

1 teaspoon prepared mustard

Paprika, salt and pepper

½ cup cream, stiffly whipped

Stir all ingredients together, fold in the whipped cream—and keep in a covered jar.

*　*　*

Being a woman who had rather stay in bed than get out of it, I do not hold with Sunday morning entertaining, and *brunch* to me is just a funny word. I say it's silly and the hell with it. But the world is filled with girls who wake with shining morning faces, bright and chipper as a dollar—and *they* can't wait to get into their little pinafores, to squeeze the oranges and broil the bacon.

A doctor told me that some people function best in

the early morning, and others later. I am one who does not function (if at all) until pretty late. My brunching experience being somewhat limited, I have talked things over with the rise-and-shine girls, and picked up a few items for the Sabbath.

The girls tell me that on Sunday mornings they have a big pitcher of orange juice on the table. And, so the juice won't get weak with ice water, they fill their ice trays the night before with tinned grapefruit or pineapple juice—and have frozen fruit cubes in the pitcher, which sounds like a right cute notion.

In Haiti, I had a cook who removed pulp and membrane from half grapefruits, sprinkled them with sugar, and over-flowed them with rum. She put them in the sun for a while, and then back on the ice to get cold—and it was such a nice way to start the day, that when I came home I did a little experimenting.

Sherry, I discovered, is equally good—or any liquor you like and happen to have around. One man I know sprinkles the grapefruit with brown sugar, dots it with butter, fills it with sherry, and puts it under a low broiler until thoroughly heated.

Pink scrambled eggs on anchovy toast are unusual and a tasty number for festive breakfast—though *plain* scrambled eggs are good enough for most men.

The great chef Escoffier, whose greatest joy was

simple dishes, made scrambled eggs famous at the Ritz in London. Before Escoffier went to the Ritz, he was chef on the Kaiser's yacht. And one day when Wilhelm was having a party, Escoffier steamed salmon in champagne, and made himself immortal.

After that, when the Duc d'Orleans was courting Madame Melba, the Duke begged Escoffier to think up a new dessert for the lady. And he thought up Pêche Melba!

Escoffier always scrambled eggs in a heavy iron pan, so that the heat reached them very slowly. But I know a slower way—and especially recommended for a party where the cook is drinking. Cook them in a double boiler—then, if you forget them for a minute (or even for thirty minutes), they won't burn. . . . And if you put a few of your little brother's marbles in the bottom of the double boiler, they will roll around and attract your wandering attention when the water boils too low.

Scrambled Eggs

Take two eggs for each person, add three tablespoons of milk for each egg, and beat with an egg beater. If you cook them directly over the flame, stir constantly. If you use a double boiler, stir occasionally. Add salt and pepper—and when they are done, a big piece of butter. Sprinkle with paprika. Serve from a hot platter, on hot plates while the butter is running in little golden streams.

I know a French girl who cooks a hearty dish for *brunch* that goes over especially well with men. She cooks pork sausages in a frying pan, and pricks them first with a fork to keep the fat from spitting. When they are *almost* but not quite done, she slips them in the oven, to keep hot—and in the pork fat that is left she sautés a chopped onion until it is golden brown. Then she pours in beaten eggs and milk, and scrambles them on top of the onion. When the eggs are scrambled, she heaps them in the center of a platter, tops them with butter, and surrounds them with sausages. And with paprika and watercress for color, the dish looks as good as it smells.

To make *Pink Scrambled Eggs* use condensed tomato soup instead of milk, and proceed as usual. Minced chives are good scrambled with eggs, and sautéd mushrooms are nice. . . . When you are in an experimental humor, remember what Brillat-Savarin said about the discovery of a new dish. Of how it does more for the happiness of mankind than the discovery of a star . . . and don't be afraid of trying unusual combinations. Once I made a Spanish Omelette with canned corn and chopped ham, plus the customary ingredients—and it was *much* better than the conventional Spanish Omelette.

Making *Anchovy Butter* for pink scrambled eggs

is the easiest thing you ever did. Get a tube of anchovy paste and a quarter of a pound of sweet butter, and cream a tablespoon or so of the paste into the butter. Be sure to get sweet butter, or it will be too salty. Paprika to color will make it pink and tasty. Butter hot toast liberally, and heap pink scrambled eggs on each slice.

A newspaper man brought me some caviar from Iceland, and it was so good I wanted to make it last, so I creamed it with sweet butter, and made it go three times as far. Cream the butter first, and whip in the caviar without crushing the little eggs. Caviar should be ice cold, and served with hot Melba toast, minced onion, and quartered lemons or limes.

Eggs are not especially exciting, but they are plenty simple, and you can invent all sorts of dishes with them. If you have individual baking dishes, bake eggs with mushrooms, crisp, minced bacon, cheese . . . or almost anything. Pour a little cream, olive oil, or melted butter in the bottom of the dish— break two eggs carefully—sprinkle with salt and pepper, and surround with the tidbits of your choice. When the whites are set, the eggs are done. Ten minutes in a slow oven is about right. Serve with toast, popovers, or baking powder biscuits.

Popovers are so simple that I learned to make them when I was eight. And when I grew up, I was surprised to learn that they are considered tricky.

Popovers
(1 dozen)

2 eggs	1 cup flour
1 cup milk	½ teaspoon each of salt and sugar

Beat eggs well, add milk and beat some more. Sift flour with salt and sugar, and add eggs and milk *gradually* to flour, stirring well—and then beat for 3 minutes with an egg beater. When I was little I strained the batter to get the lumps out, but now there are no lumps in it, and I suppose it is because I beat harder. Butter muffin tins—iron ones are best—and place in a hot oven (450°) for 20 minutes. Reduce the heat (to 350°), and bake 15 to 20 minutes more.

For Sunday breakfasts, when I was a small girl and didn't mind getting up in the morning, I used to make Baking Powder Biscuits.

Baking Powder Biscuits

2 cups sifted flour	5 tablespoons of butter,
4 teaspoons baking powder	Spry or Crisco
½ teaspoon salt	¾ cup milk

Sift flour with baking powder and salt, and work in shortening with your finger tips, or cut it in with a knife, until the mixture is fine as meal. Add milk, and mix well. Drop dough on floured board, flour lightly, and roll quickly to half-inch thickness. Cut with small biscuit cutter as quickly as possible. The secret of good biscuits is not to handle them. Place on cookie sheet, or inverted cake tin, and bake in a hot oven (450°) for about 15 minutes. This will make 18 small biscuits.

Tomatoes go well with eggs, and in the summertime they are so inexpensive that it is good to use lots of them. To skin tomatoes quickly and neatly, stick a fork in the bud end and hold over a flame for a minute—or dip quickly in boiling water. To keep them from cooking to pieces, slice in two, and sear both sides quickly in an iron frying pan. If you do this, you might put the seared slices in a little baking dish, drop an egg or two carefully on top. Adorn with slivers of mushroom or bacon, and bake.

Mary Barber, the famous dietician who plans meals for the Army and knows what men like, recommends:

Tomatoes Michael
(for six)

6 or 8 tomatoes
Seasoned flour (she means *season* it)
2 tablespoons butter or bacon fat
Speck of baking soda
2 tablespoons sugar
½ cup heavy cream

Wash, peel and slice tomatoes. Dredge with seasoned flour. Melt butter or bacon in heavy frying pan, add tomatoes, and sauté until well browned on both sides. As tomatoes brown, transfer to another pan. Add more fat when necessary. When all slices are browned, stir together until well mixed. Stir in soda, sugar, and cream, and cook over low heat until well blended.

* * *

I just read an Associated Press story that says Grace Moore is a good cook and has boasted about it ever since her Brownies won first prize at the Jacksboro, Tenn. county fair. (She won third prize for her singing at the same fair.) I am going to give you a recipe for Brownies that are so good they'd make even Miss Moore take notice. But first I want to tell you about *Rainbow Chicken.*

Chapter Twelve

Bachelor Bait-

There is a terrible chapter in my life in which I owned a tearoom in Wellesley called the *Rainbow,* that began in a blaze of glory and ended in a terrible flop.

In the booths were satin cushions, all colors of the rainbow. And the waitresses wore aprons and caps to match. China and glasses came in six hues, and variegated flowers filled multi-colored bowls. There were rainbow curtains at the windows, the walls were painted sixteen shades. And everything was as dizzy as a kaleidoscope, and as gay as confetti.

For three months business was wonderful, and the customers stood and waited like lambs. . . . Then, suddenly, things went sour. The manager got sick, the cook got drunk, the dishwasher got fallen arches . . . and I got stuck.

When the cook was plastered, the *Rainbow's* glory was shed. When the help was scattered, my joy in the place lay dead. . . . And the thing that kept me awake nights was a *specialité de la maison* which was something like Chicken a la King, only it took three hours to cook the hens.

Tearoom etiquette decrees that hens be called *chickens,* but a meaty bird with heavy legs, and a plump breast, is no chicken. We used ten or a dozen of them each day, and when I pinched hit for the cook, I took the creatures home at midnight, to cook in the laundry. I put them on at one, and a newspaperman who worked nights telephoned at four, for me to get up and take them off. This went on for nine months, and it was a long time after I closed the *Rainbow* before I could look a hen in the face.

The alleged chicken, however, was delicious and I am going to tell you how I fixed it, because a *Rainbow Chicken Dinner* is something you can get ready the day before, and the longer it stands the better it is. If you are a working girl, Monday is a good night for a party, because you get things set on Sunday, and on Monday run them off with the greatest of ease—the clever young girl on the flying trapeze!

Rainbow Chicken

1 plump fowl	½ pound mushrooms
1 bunch of celery	1 small green pepper
3 onions	1 small can pimentos
2 or 3 carrots	1 jar cream
1 kernel of garlic	Butter
6 tablespoons flour	Salt and pepper

Have the butcher clean the fowl, and save the fat and innards. If your particular hen hasn't much fat on her, ask for some more. Keep her whole, put her in a kettle, and cover with water. Add the tops of the celery, and a few of the outside pieces; onions, peeled and quartered; garlic, carrots, innards, and seasoning. Bring quickly to a boil, and simmer gently for about three hours, or until the old hen is as tender as a chicken. The French have a nice expression for simmering—they say *keep the pot smiling*. . . . When the fowl is done, take it out of the pot to cool. Strain the stock . . . and there's your nice soup.

Wash the chicken fat and try it out in an iron skillet, or in the top of the boiler. The double boiler business takes longer, but is not smoky . . . or you can try it out in the oven. Since I do not know how much liquid fat you will get, I'll have to tell you to use it with common sense, and if you haven't enough, use butter. Make a cream gravy by mixing the flour with some of the fat, and when they are nicely blended, add a cup of the clear chicken stock and then a jar of cream, stir-

ring constantly over a low flame. This will make a
rich cream gravy (the chicken fat makes it yellow).
Now sauté the mushrooms, stems and all, in some
more of the fat, or in butter if the fat is gone. Mushrooms cook quickly, since they are mostly water. Chop
the green pepper and a stalk or two of the celery and
cook for ten minutes in just enough boiling water to
keep them from burning. (Save the heart of the celery
to stuff with roquefort or cream cheese, for hors
d'œuvres.) Add mushrooms, pepper and celery to the
gravy, and pimentos cut in pieces. If you wish, you
may also add diced canned pineapple . . . or omit
celery, peppers, pimentos, and fruit. . . . One of the
first things for a beginner to learn is that it is often
possible to add to or subtract from any given recipe.

Save enough of the chicken for a sandwich or two,
cut the rest in sizeable chunks, and add to the gravy.
Pour everything in the top of the double boiler, and
stick in the refrigerator until tomorrow.

At the *Rainbow* we had a girl who went to Gar-
land School and studied at Miss Farmer's. She
used to pretty up the plates before they went to the
dining room. For color effect and "appetite appeal," she would cross strips of green pepper and
red pimento on top of each serving. She gave practically everything a dash of paprika, and stuck sprigs
of parsley in the tops of the stuffed potatoes. A girl
can do a lot with a bunch of parsley and a tin of
paprika—but don't be too fussy! . . . Once I went to
a luncheon where the hostess dolled up the lamb

chops in lingerie, and by the time they reached the table, they were shivering in their little petticoats.

Baked potatoes should be hot and flaky, and pinched open to let the steam escape. A gob of butter should be popped in the slit, and maybe a piece of cheese. And the top sprinkled with paprika. Rather than let potatoes get cold and soggy, you might bake and stuff them the day before, to slide in the oven the last minute. Buy Idaho Jumbos, and get them all of a size. Never use new potatoes for baking. Scrub well, wipe dry, and rub with cooking oil, fat, or butter. Pre-heat the oven until it is pretty hot (450°), and bake from 40 to 60 minutes, depending upon the size of the potatoes.

Stuffed Potatoes

While the potatoes are still hot, slice off the broadest sides, and scoop them out. Mash well, add a bit of finely minced onion or chopped chives, a very generous piece of butter, warm cream (top-of-the-bottle will do), a beaten egg, salt and pepper . . . and beat until your arm is tired. Heap back into the shells, cover with a fresh napkin, and set aside until tomorrow.

Rainbow Peas

Follow directions on the package of frozen peas— only use clear chicken soup, instead of water. Toss in a lump of sugar—and if there is lettuce around, shred the heart, and add that. When the peas are done, season with salt and pepper and a soupçon of grated nutmeg—and drown in butter.

*   *   *

If you are a barbecue enthusiast, I don't have to tell you how to broil a steak because you have been broiling them all summer—and I hope you knew enough to get them an inch and a half thick.

Way back in the Gas and Electrical Age, I tried to encourage people to cook over charcoal. In *Ports Of The Sun,* I talked about buying coal pots in the West Indies. I told apprehensive amateurs they could get a handful of charcoal, and broil steaks, chicken and lobsters to make themselves famous.

I used my coal pot in the garden at home. And one winter in New York, I used it in the bath tub. I think I was the first woman in America to own one. And now you'd think there wouldn't be room in peoples' lives for the barbecue equipment they have! Grills come all the way up to $60, and pretty darn fancy . . . but I am sticking with my 75 cent coal pot.

When I broil steak or hamburgers, I toast thick slices of bread over the coals, and slather them with butter. But since some people feel that potatoes form a pattern with steak, I am going to give you a recipe for Delmonico Potatoes from the Hotel Touraine in Boston, which is famous for them.

Delmonico Potatoes
(for two)

3 average potatoes	½ teaspoon salt
1 jar light cream	Dash of nutmeg and white
2 tablespoons butter	pepper
½ cup Cheddar cheese	

Chop boiled potatoes very fine and cook gently for 5 minutes with cream, butter, and seasoning. Pour in a shallow pan and cover with grated cheese. Place under broiler until cheese melts and is brown (about 3 minutes).

*   *   *

A French chef once told me that he and his colleagues thought out elegant dishes, worked from special recipes, fiddled with weights and thermometers . . . and never in their lives turned out anything as good as Hamburgers.

Last summer I had dinner with a couple who cook on an Abercrombie & Fitch grill, in a penthouse with a rose garden and a butler . . . and the dinner they like best is *Hamburgers.* Maury slivers a kernel of garlic, minces an onion, mixes with chopped sirloin, adds salt and pepper, and binds with light cream.

Garlic (in genteel moderation) is one of the flavors I am fondest of. I have read that the ancient Egyptians had a positive lust for it, and tried (unsuccessfully, I'll bet) to hide their passion from the priests, who regarded it as a most unclean abomination. . . . I used to slit steak and chops, and slip in garlic to flavor them while broiling. But this concentrated the flavor, and I recently read a better idea. Grate a clove or two of garlic in a few tablespoons of olive oil or melted butter, and smear the surface of the meat with a pastry brush.

Sauce for Hamburgers
(for two)

3 medium size tomatoes	1 small green pepper
2 small onions	½ pound mushrooms
2 tablespoons butter	1 tablespoon flour
1 teaspoon Worcestershire	Plenty of seasoning

Sauté chopped onions in butter, and sauté mushrooms in some more butter. When the onions are quite yellow, add chopped peppers, peeled tomatoes, and flour. Cook for ten minutes. Add mushrooms, and cook a little longer.*

Mushroom sauce is good with a number of things, and should be in your repertory.

Mushroom Sauce

½ pound mushrooms	2 tablespoons flour
3 tablespoons butter	A jigger of sherry
1 cup light cream	Salt and pepper

Wash and slice the mushrooms and sauté in butter. Season, and dredge with flour. Add cream, stirring

* This also makes a good Spanish Omelette.

constantly, and when thick and smooth, add sherry (if
you like sherry).

*   *   *

When a girl makes a play for a man, he can see
what's coming. Men spot the bait from a long way
off, and have plenty of chance to shy away, if they
don't like it. But many of them are ready to get
hooked—and if the bait is nice, they'll take it with
both eyes open—take it and love it.

Burgundy Beef Stew makes lovely bait, and if
you should get a quart of California Burgundy,
you'd have enough left over to serve at dinner.
Make the stew the night before. Most dishes are
better if the ingredients become familiar with one
another—and there's nothing like a night in the
refrigerator.

Burgundy Beef Stew
(for two)

1 pound lean beef	1 small parsnip
3 onions	½ eggplant
3 stalks celery	1 or 2 cloves of garlic
3 or 4 little peeled carrots	½ pound mushrooms
2 tablespoons concentrated	½ bay leaf
tomato soup	Salt, pepper, and a bit of
4 tablespoons flour	thyme and marjoram

1 cup California red wine

Cook mushroom stems with the meat, and save the
caps for the gravy. Have the beef cut in inch squares,

and ask the butcher for a piece of suet. Try out the suet, and brown the beef in the fat. If you can't get suet, use Crisco, Spry, or butter. Add the vegetables cut small, and the seasoning. Sprinkle with flour, and turn with a spoon until everything is well mixed. Pour in the wine, and stir—then stir in the tomato, and bring to a boil: Cover the dish and place in a hot oven. Let it cook for two and a half hours— then taste the meat to see if it is very tender. And if it isn't, let it cook a while longer. After the meat has been taken out, strain the gravy, pressing the vegetables through a strainer until you have extracted all the good that's in them.

Before serving, sauté the mushroom caps in butter, and when they are almost done, add the meat—cover tightly and keep on a low burner while you heat the gravy. Pour the gravy over meat and mushrooms, and serve very hot.

*   *   *

The thing I make best is Lobster Newburg, and if I do say so as shouldn't, it is extraordinarily good . . . and I am not the only one who says so, either. Before I learned to make it, I was a ravenous customer at the Copley Plaza in Boston, where I asked, one night, if I might go to the kitchen to watch the chef.

Up to this night the Copley Plaza had a reputation for the best Lobster Newburg in the East . . . First, the chef sautéd the lobster in sweet butter, then he cooked it in sherry. He made a sauce, and added an egg. And it was all very complicated and delicious. And when it was done, we went to the dining room, and ate a chafing dish full.

The next day I bought lobster meat, Harvey's Bristol Cream Sherry, and some sweet butter . . . and that night *I* made the best Lobster Newburg in the East! . . . and if Mr. Wenburg could have smelled it, he would have sat up in his grave to beg for a taste.

Mr. Wenburg invented Lobster Wenburg. He invented it one night at Delmonico's, and it became a Delmonico speciality, until the day Mr. Wenburg quarreled with Mr. Delmonico—and Mr. Delmonico changed the name. I can't give you the Wenburg version, and my own is incredibly simple and un-professional. For a while I made it with sweet butter, but one night when I didn't have any sweet butter, I used salted—and it was so nearly identical, that now I use whichever is handier. And I *never* sauté the lobster, or cook it in sherry (as chefs do) because I think it makes the lobster tough.

Lobster Newburg
(for two)

Meat of 2 medium-sized lobsters	2 biggish tablespoons flour
1 jar cream	Salt and pepper
3 tablespoons butter	1 jigger of Sherry
	Paprika

Tell the fishman you want the shells for a bisque, and ask him for an extra shell or two.

Melt butter in the top of the double boiler, and add the flour. Blend smoothly and add cream and seasoning, stirring constantly. When thick and very hot, add the lobster meat, which you have cut in nice big chunks. (Save the coral and green part for bisque). At the last, pour in the sherry—and sprinkle liberally with paprika.

This may be eaten at once, or may be kept hot in the double boiler, but turn the heat off. Too much cooking makes lobster tough.

If there is any Lobster Newburg left (but I am sure there won't be), it will keep in the refrigerator for a day or two, and makes grand canapés. Toast rounds of bread on one side. Butter the untoasted side, heap with lobster, and put under the broiler for a moment. If it stays too long, it will run and get messy. Maybe it would be safer, to serve it cold on crisp crackers.

Lobster Bisque
(for two)

Break the shells and put them on to boil with 1½ cups of cold water and an onion. There is no sense using the big empty claws, but only the backs and the small claws. Simmer gently for 15 or 20 minutes.

Meanwhile take the green part (I think it's the liver, but it's all right, whatever it is), and crush it with the coral (the coral is pink, and comes only in female lobsters, because it is eggs). Blend with butter and flour, and make a cream sauce with a cup of light cream. Strain in the lobster stock, season to taste, cook for a few minutes in the top of the double boiler, and just before serving, add a jigger of sherry and a dash of paprika.

Garlic intrudes in my cooking so often that I think I had better reassure you about it. If you really *eat* garlic, you are going to smell something *awful*. But if you use it with discretion you can live in harmony with the nicest people. When using a single clove, mince it, so that it will be thoroughly dissolved in cooking. When using more than one, split each one lengthwise. Run a toothpick through each piece (for identification), and remove while still intact. Keep a few kernels in jars of mayonnaise, olives and pickles—but be careful they never get to the table.

A *good* Curry is a fine one-dish meal—and no fuss with salad or vegetables. Some girls (nice girls, too—but *terrible* cooks) simply add curry powder to a thin white sauce. Curry connoisseurs adopt a procedure that takes hours. And they are both extremists who ruin either the dish or the day.

The success of a curry does not exactly *depend* upon a coconut, but I hope you can get one. If you can't, use light cream. There are all sorts of curries

—lamb, veal, chicken, and seafoods. But shrimp is easiest, and least expensive. I have tried fresh shrimps and imported prawns, and I prefer the little tins that come from chain stores. Remove that little black strip that runs down their backs, because it's their digestive tracts. And don't open the cans until you are going to use them. But everything else can be prepared the night before.

Get the coconut, if you can, two days ahead, and have the market man split it open, and save the milk for you. Put the coconut meat through the chopper (a food chopper is something a girl really should have). Cover the ground meat with water, and place in the refrigerator over night, or longer. Then squeeze it through a cheese cloth until you get every drop of juice. Add this to the milk that was in the nut, and you probably will have about a pint.

Curry Sauce

Milk of 1 coconut (or about a pint of light cream)	1 teaspoon sugar
	1 chopped onion
½ cup butter (=¼ lb.)	1 big cooking apple
3 tablespoons flour	1 garlic clove
2 tablespoons curry powder	Salt and pepper

Cook the onion, sliced apple, and a little garlic in the butter. (O. O. McIntyre used to say there's no such thing as a little garlic.) Some people cook a banana, a small diced carrot, and a stalk or two of celery with the onion and apple—and also a little piece of fresh ginger root. When you get to be a good cook, you will add and subtract, as you please—not only when you cook a curry, but practically anything. Meantime, just add what you please to the butter, and when it is pulpy, press through a sieve. Blend with curry, sugar, flour and seasoning, and add gradually the coconut milk, or cream, stirring constantly over slow fire. All sauces are richer if a piece of butter is added before serving.

Heat shrimps in a little of the sauce, and keep the rest very hot, to serve on the side.

Fried bananas are good with curry. Split lengthwise, and fry quickly in butter. Or– to have them ready ahead of time– place in a shallow tin, with butter—sprinkle with brown sugar and lemon juice, and bake until soft. For color, sprinkle with paprika.

Serve the Curry in a casserole, with a bowl of hot flaky rice on the side, the bananas on a hot platter, a pitcher of extra sauce, and an array of accompaniments. When serving, place a banana on the plate, then rice, and top with curried shrimps. Let everyone help himself to relishes, and to the pitcher of curry sauce.

Fill an hors d'oeuvres tray (or just some saucers) with condiments. A tin of Bombay duck is considered pretty smart, but it's nothing but dried fish— and you are supposed to toast, crush, and crumble it. Chopped peanuts or cashew nuts are good, and also crisp, crumbled bacon. Fresh shredded coconut is

excellent. And you should have Chutney, of course
—Major Gray's is the best, I think. It is quite an
accomplishment to run off a Curry Party, and you'd
better have a dress rehearsal with the family first—
after which it will be a cinch.*

Rice

Rice is an inviting dish if given half a chance, but
the pasty-white and sticky way some people serve
it is simply revolting. Before I ever knew that
Mexicans fry rice, I turned out something rather
special. I dropped half a cup of uncooked rice into
some hot olive oil, and stirred until it was golden
brown. (An iron frying pan is best for this.) Then
I poured the browned rice into a sauce pan of madly
boiling salted water, and when it was almost done
and the water had boiled nearly away, I added a cup
of hot chicken stock and boiled it some more . . .
and it was simply delicious.

Rice drinks up an astonishing amount of water—
use eight or ten times as much boiling water as rice,
and even then you'll have to keep your mind on it.

Here is a tasty dish that requires a double boiler for
safety's sake. First fry the raw rice—half a cup of
it, then add a can of tomato paste, a chopped onion,

* If you are in New York, go to the *East India Curry Shop* (a
restaurant and store combined) at 122 East 57th Street. Have dinner
first—and then buy the accompaniments you like best, to serve at home.

a minced clove of garlic, and maybe a chopped green pepper, half a bay leaf, plenty of salt and a good dash of pepper. Cook directly over the flame for five minutes, stirring constantly. Add three cups of hot soup stock, if you have it—or boiling water, if you haven't. And cook in double boiler for an hour. Good with almost anything.

*　　*　　*

A girl I know fell in love with a newspaper man who lived in a rooming house, and ate in bars. And hardly ever had a home-made bite. She knew that if she asked him to dinner he would shy off, because he was a bachelor who knew all the tricks. So she took to bringing funny-looking parcels to the office, and parking them, accidently-on-purpose, on his desk. Being a curious guy, he asked questions.

"Bundles for Britain, Nancy?"

"Oh, no—that's stuff for a curry, and some strawberries—I'm going to make a shortcake when I get home."

This went on for quite a while, and Nancy wasn't throwing any money away on fancy groceries. One morning she'd wrap up a couple pair of rubbers—the next, some overshoes and a few books—in stout manila paper, with cord from a fancy grocery. Finally the hungry reporter could stand it no longer.

"Who do you do all this cooking for?" he demanded.

"Oh it depends—people I like."

"How about me?" . . . So she asked him out for dinner . . . and they lived happily ever after.

* * *

In the last chapter I said that most men like ham, and now I am going to give you a specialty of the famous Toll House. The Wakefields, who own the Toll House, tell me that it is *especially popular with men*. Get the best vacuum-packed ham, and what you don't use now, you can use in some sandwiches that I'll tell you about in a minute.

Ham Baked with Cheese

Slice a thick piece of ham, place it in a casserole, and pour over it a cup of rich cream sauce in which you have melted half a pound of American cheese. The sauce should be well seasoned with cayenne and paprika, half a teaspoon of dry mustard, a dash of Worcestershire, and a couple of tablespoons of lemon juice. Bake uncovered until cheese is slightly brown.

An excellent accompaniment for Ham (or Fried Chicken) is a Corn Pudding, and here is a recipe I gave in *An Island Patchwork*. A woman wrote me that if I left out the milk, sugar and flour, and added a half cup of maple syrup, and didn't separate the eggs, it would be better, but I don't like a vegetable pudding on the sweet side, so I haven't tried it.

Nantucket Corn Pudding
(à la mode)

1 pint can of corn	1 pint milk
3 eggs	2 tablespoons flour
4 tablespoons melted butter	1 tablespoon sugar
ter	Salt and pepper

Beat the yolks of the eggs, add other ingredients, and fold in the stiffly beaten whites. Pour in a covered casserole and place in a pan of hot water. Bake slowly for an hour (350°). If the water in the pan bubbles, the custard may curdle, so add a little cold water occasionally.

There are two ways of using the rest of that tinned ham. One of them was given me by Oscar of the Waldorf, and so I call it:

Oscar Himself

Bread	2 eggs
Slices of Ham, Chicken, and Swiss Cheese	A little cream
	Salt and pepper
Plenty of butter	

Remove crusts and butter well two slices of bread. Place between them one slice of ham, three of chicken, and two thin slices of Swiss cheese. Beat two eggs slightly with a little cream and seasoning, and pour mixture in a platter. Now soak the sandwiches, and when they are nicely saturated, fry them in melted butter until the cheese starts to melt.

Dill pickles and coffee are the best things to serve with sandwiches.

Kentucky Special

Bread	Butter
Ham ·	Orange juice
Bananas	Brown sugar

Toast one side of bread, and butter the other. Then cover untoasted side with slices of cold ham, and top with banana, cut lengthwise and then quartered. Brush with melted butter, sprinkle lightly with brown sugar and orange juice, and brown under broiler.

*   *   *

While you have cold cuts around, you might like to toss up a Potato Salad. I have a superior recipe from a girl called Bea who does very well with the boys, and modestly attributes her success to her cooking.

Potato Salad

6 medium sized potatoes (boiled in their jackets)	½ cup chopped stuffed olives
2 hard-boiled eggs	1 onion, made to *weep*
3 strips bacon broiled very crisp	2 tablespoons minced green pepper
½ cup diced celery	Pepper and sugar

It is better to use onion juice in a salad than even the tiniest pieces, because hardly anyone likes to get raw onion between his teeth. You can buy onion juice, but it isn't as good as what you'll get if you make an onion *weep*. To do this, cut the onion in halves and soak each half in salt—then run a knife over the salted portion and scrape out the juice. If you spear the onion on a fork, you can manage without getting your fingers smelly. . . . But if you *do* get onion (or garlic) on your fingers, the quickest way to get the smell off, is to wash your hands with soap, and then rub your fingers with a lime.

Peel and cut potatoes in large dice. Mash bacon with a fork. Slice eggs. Toss all ingredients together with enough mayonnaise to moisten, add pepper, and a good pinch of sugar. Serve in mounds on crisp lettuce. Garnish with radish roses, or wedges of ripe tomato, and sprinkle liberally with paprika.

*   *   *

Do you remember that $2500 Soufflé I mentioned? Well, Soufflé is something else that goes well with cold cuts. The boy who gave me this recipe runs an unusual eating place in Boston. His name is Edmund Stanley, and more than anything else, Edmund once wanted a piano. He bought three glass casters from the five-and-ten, and placed them on the drawing-room floor, and then he started figuring. The piano he wanted cost $2500.

He propositioned seven people and offered them dinner for a dollar, in the paneled basement of the little house in which he lived. It would take two and a half years to meet the piano payments, if the

seven accepted . . . and the seven *did* accept. And
Edmund ordered the piano, and put it on the casters.

At this writing there are two payments left, and
Edmund's fame rests on his Cheese Soufflé. It is a
good thing to serve for late supper, or on Sunday
evening when everyone has had a big noon-day dinner. And the only out is that it *must be eaten at
once*—or it will fall.

Cheese Soufflé
(for a crowd)

1 tall can Borden's evaporated milk	6 tablespoons flour
	6 eggs
Water	1 teaspoon salt
Package of Cheddar Cheese	½ teaspoon mustard
2 tablespoons Spry	

Dump into a quart jar the can of milk with flour
and seasoning, and shake vigorously. Melt Spry in
saucepan, pour in evaporated milk, fill the empty can
with water and add that. Then the cheese, cut in
pieces. Stir constantly, and when the cheese is melted,
cool mixture slightly, and add beaten egg yolks. Then
fold in the whites, beaten stiffly with three teaspoons
of water. Bake in a thick, huge casserole for an hour
and a half.

*   *   *

I feel about my Rabbit the way I do about my
Newburg. It is so simple, you probably won't believe it. And it is not orthodox at all . . . but very

good. And it is the only recipe I know that *cannot* get rubbery.

Foolproof Rabbit
(for four)

1 jar light cream	1 teaspoon mustard
1 pound Cheddar or good old American Cheese (I dislike processed cheeses)	2 tablespoons flour
	Red pepper and salt
	1 egg yolk

Make a white sauce in the top of the double boiler, with plenty of seasoning, and add the cheese, cut in small pieces. When smooth and creamy, add beaten yolk and cook a little longer. Serve on Melba toast, with a hunk of butter and a dash of paprika on top. You can use the whole egg if you want, but the white will make the rabbit a bit fluffy.

A friend who makes a wonderful *Irish Rabbit* uses Guinness Dublin Stout. In a chafing dish or double boiler, he blends 2 tablespoons of butter, two tablespoons of flour, and half a teaspoon of salt. He adds half a cup of milk, and cooks until thick, stirring constantly. Then he adds a pound of chopped American cheese, and stirs until melted. After which, he blends in three-fourths of a cup of Guinness Stout, and keeps on stirring. This makes four to six servings—and is very good, but not so easy to make as mine.

A good toast spread is easily made by melting a package of cheese in a can of concentrated tomato soup. If you have a bottle of stuffed olives, slice them in—or some sautéd mushrooms. Serve on crackers if you prefer—and use plenty of butter and paprika. . . . To keep cheese forever, put it in a covered jar, with a few lumps of sugar—and it won't mold, or get stale.

* * *

Then love was the pearl of his oyster,
And Venus rose red out of wine.

Panned oysters are rather sophisticated with a green salad and good for a late supper. You can use fresh oysters, of course—but if you live away from the seacoast, you'd better get a box of the frozen kind, and allow a couple hours for them to thaw. One of the best things about oysters is that it doesn't take ten minutes to do things with them (after they are thawed).

Panned Oysters

1 package oysters	½ cup chili sauce
¼ pound butter	Salt and pepper
½ teaspoon Worcestershire	Melba toast
½ cup heavy cream	

Thaw the oysters, and saute gently in their own liquid and melted butter, until their edges begin to curl. Add seasonings, chili, and cream. Heat thoroughly, and serve on Melba toast. (Melba toast comes in packages.)

Oysters are supposed to be an aphrodisiac—but don't count on it.

Chapter Thirteen

Since Eve Ate Apples

All human history attests
That happiness for man—the hungry sinner!—
Since Eve ate apples, much depends on dinner.

Make a sinner happy! . . . and a good dessert may lead to who-knows-what?

The crowning touch to an excellent dinner is a perfect dessert. Young men usually prefer a sweet—older men like cheese, or a savory. Ice cream is considered a bit gauche (though I don't know why, and I wouldn't care). Fruits are Continental—savories, smart. And apple pie à la mode is American.

*　　*　　*

When I was living in the West Indies, I received some northern apples from home. Auxanges had never tasted apples, and I showed her how to make a New England Pandowdy.

"It suah do hit de spot," she murmured, rubbing same, and rolling her eyes ecstatically.

Auxanges was worried because I was not married.

"When crab hab no hole, she nebber get fat," she used to sigh, meaning that home life is best for a woman.

But the Pandowdy settled matters.

"Miss," she said, "Ah ain' worried 'bout youah no moah. When God A'mighty smell dat dowdy, he goin' send youah de beses' man He got."

Years ago my grandmother had some strawberry shortcake that she considered extraordinarily good. The woman who made it went to Florida, and Grandmother wrote for the recipe. This made an impression on her children, and when it arrived and the family tried it out, they christened it *Thousand Mile Shortcake.* It is almost like Baking Powder Biscuits, and is equally good for either Shortcake or Dowdy . . . but for *Dowdy,* you use only half of it, and you don't have to roll it.

For *Shortcake,* add more flour (or use less milk) so that the dough won't be too sticky to handle— but never use more flour than you have to. Cook in two round tins. And when it is done, put sweetened crushed strawberries and a little whipped cream between. And *lots* of whipped cream and whole berries on top.

Stylish, new-fangled Shortcake calls for more shortening and less baking powder, and is made in thin individual biscuits . . . which is all right for girls on a diet. But men (*the hungry sinners*) prefer it bounteous and old-fashioned—cut in big wedges, with cream spilling over.

Thousand Mile Biscuit Dough for Pandowdy
(For Shortcake, Double Recipe)

1 cup flour	¼ teaspoon salt
2 teaspoons baking powder	1 teaspoon sugar
3 tablespoons shortening	¼ cup milk
1 egg	1 teaspoon vanilla

Mix as for biscuits, sifting sugar with flour. Add vanilla to milk. Beat egg slightly . . . and beat mixture well. Spread with a spoon over apples.

5 tart apples	1 tablespoon butter
½ teaspoon cinnamon	Biggish pinch of salt
½ cup brown sugar	¼ cup boiling water

Peel and cut apples in eighths. Add water. Mix cinnamon and salt with sugar, and sprinkle over apples. Dot with butter, and cover with dough. Bake in hot oven (450°) 10 minutes then reduce heat to moderate (350°), and bake for half an hour longer, or until apples are tender.

Sauce for Pandowdy

1 cup confectioner's sugar   1 teaspoon flavoring
½ cup butter   ,   ⅛ teaspoon salt

Cream butter first, and then cream everything together. For flavoring, use vanilla or almond extract—
or a dash of rum, if you like it. A hard sauce should
be thoroughly chilled before serving . . . and I have
been meaning to tell you that when recipes call for
brown sugar, they almost always mean *dark* brown.

Another good apple dessert is *Brown Betty*. Men
scorn sissy foods, but there is nothing sissy about a
Betty but its name, and the boys go for it.

Brown Betty

6 tart apples   1 teaspoon grated lemon
1 cup water   rind
¼ cup granulated sugar   3 tablespoons   chopped
½ cup brown sugar   walnuts
3 tablespoons butter   ½ teaspoon cinnamon
10 graham crackers   Pinch of salt

Peel, core and quarter apples, and cook in water
until they are almost but not quite tender (if you cook
them too long, they will go to mush in the Betty). Add
sugar, stirring so as not to crush the apples. Pour
into a buttered shallow baking dish. Roll graham
crackers lightly—*don't* powder them—the crumbs
should be coarse. Sprinkle over the apples—and then
sprinkle crumbs with brown sugar, in which you have
mixed cinnamon, lemon rind, salt and walnuts. Bake

in a hot oven (450°) for about 20 minutes, or until the top is brown and crusty.

Brown Betty is delicious with plain heavy cream, whipped cream, or hard sauce.

*   *   *

The trouble with most Brownies is they are baked too long. They should be a bit on the messy side— soft, sticky and sweet. This recipe I used when I was a thrifty child, and peddled Brownies to my relatives, who were willing enough to pay for them since they were better than anything they could buy.

Brownies

1 cup sugar	2 squares chocolate
⅓ cup butter	Scant ½ cup flour
2 eggs	½ cup chopped walnuts
	1 teaspoon vanilla

Melt butter and mix with sugar. Add unbeaten eggs, one at a time . . . and stir considerably. Melt chocolate over hot water, add, and stir some more. Then add sifted flour, a speck of salt, and vanilla, and keep on stirring. Spread in a buttered cake pan (10 by 7 inches), and bake in a slow oven for about 15 minutes. Maybe it will take 20 minutes, but test at 15 with a toothpick or broom straw, and if it comes out nice and sticky—but not doughy—the Brownies are done. Cut in squares while warm.

*   *   *

People who read my books and know I like to cook, sometimes send me recipes. And a man in Newark wrote about the wonderful *Egg Nog Pie* his wife makes. It was so good, he wanted me to try it—and, gallantly, he enclosed the recipe. So this morning I tried it . . . and it curdled.

Now it happened that the other evening, I had dinner with a friend who served what *she* called *Chiffon Pie*. When mine curdled, I telephoned to ask her how hers was made. She conferred at great length with her cook, and finally called me back. And then I made *another* pie . . . and *that* one curdled too!

By this time I had spoiled two elegant pie shells, that I had baked, one by one. Then I called Marjorie Mills, Woman's Page editor of the *Boston Herald,* who is famous for her reliable recipes, to ask what could the matter be.

And Marjorie said, "Why, Eleanor Early, the best recipe there is for Rum Chiffon Pie is the one they make at the Statler, that you quoted in your *New England Sampler."*

So I looked it up—and here it is. The reason I had forgotten it, was that I'd eaten it so often at the hotel, I *knew* it was good, and when the chef gave me the recipe, I didn't bother checking on it, the way I usually do. But now I have made it—and it's *foolproof!* . . . Cooking rum dispels alcoholic content, and only the flavor remains—so that this is a pie you can serve with propriety to your W. C. T. U. aunt.

Rum Chiffon Pie

3 egg yolks		¼ cup cold water
½ cup sugar		3 egg whites
½ cup rum		½ cup additional sugar
1 tablespoon	granulated	Pinch of salt
gelatin		

Beat egg yolks, add sugar and rum, and cook in a double boiler until they make a soft custard. Soak the gelatin in cold water, and place over boiling tea kettle, to dissolve. Beat the egg whites with the additional sugar. If you use a sweet, heavy rum, like Jamaican, you probably won't need this extra sugar. I used Barcardi, and used only two extra spoonsful. You might need more . . . it all depends on the rum. But however much or little you use, you can't spoil *this* recipe! When the egg whites begin to hold shape, pour the gelatin in slowly, beating all the time. By this time, the custard should be cool—but if it isn't, wait until it does cool . . . *this is very important!* Then fold the custard in the light and fluffy eggs, and pour into a baked pie shell. Top with *slightly* sweetened whipped cream, and serve very cold.

There are two ways of making pie crust—one with ice water, and the other with boiling water—but the best one for a shell is made with hot water and comes out very flaky—*too* flaky for a two-crust pie.

Flaky Pie Crust

¼ cup shortening   1 cup flour
3 tablespoons boiling water   ½ teaspoon salt
          ¼ teaspoon baking powder

Pour boiling water over shortening, and beat with
a fork. Sift flour with baking powder and salt. Stir
liquid into flour. Roll, and shape to pie plate. Place in
refrigerator to chill—and keep it there as long as you
want. I usually make mine the day before. Bake in
a preheated hot oven until lightly brown—about fifteen
minutes. An easy way to measure shortening is to fill
a measuring cup three quarters full of water, and then
drop the shortening in until the water overflows.

*   *   *

Hortense Odlum, the famous lady who became
President of Bonwit Teller's in its lean days, and
made it one of the smartest shops in New York, has
a recipe for Apple Sauce Cake that she makes for
her two boys. It is a mannish sort of cake because
it has a cheese frosting. And it is awfully easy, because it is made with canned apple sauce.

Apple Sauce Cake

½ cup shortening   1 teaspoon soda
1 cup brown sugar   ½ teaspoon nutmeg
1 egg, beaten   1 teaspoon cinnamon
1 cup fresh or canned   ¾ cup seedless raisins
   applesauce   Pinch of salt
1¾ cups sifted cake flour

Cream butter until soft. Blend in brown sugar. Add egg, beating until light. Stir in applesauce. Mix and sift dry ingredients, combine with raisins, and stir into first mixture. Turn into a buttered (8-inch) loaf pan; and bake in a moderate oven (350°), about 45 minutes. Cool and frost with

Cream Cheese Frosting

2 (3-ounce) packages cream cheese
⅛ teaspoon salt

About 3 cups confectioner's sugar
¼ cup top-of-the-bottle milk

Use just enough sugar to make a nice consistency, and spread with a knife.

* * *

Ice cream is an easy dessert, if you have an electric refrigerator. And if you buy it at Schrafft's or the drugstore, it's even easier.

A can of big black cherries heated in their syrup makes a grand sauce—and is grander if you add a jigger of brandy, or rum. Brandied red cherries are also good—and as good cold as hot.

Rainbow Sauce

½ pound caramels   1 jar cream

Put together in the upper part of the double boiler, and wait until the caramels melt. This is richer than any boughten syrup, and was a great favorite with Wellesley College girls.

* * *

Now I am going to tell you how to make *Meringue Shells,* because there are occasions when a Dowdy would be just too commonplace, and a girl likes to serve something Ritzy. Maybe Meringues aren't *really* Ritzy . . . maybe I only think they are, because, in the old days when the Ritz was the only place in Paris for decent American ice cream, it was always served on top of meringues.

Madame Ritz was living at the hotel then, and she told me about her husband Caesar, who was born a peasant in Switzerland—became a waiter in Paris—and lived to make his name *ritzy!* Caesar saved his tips and went in business for himself. First in Paris, then in London—and, by and by, all over Europe and North America. Escoffier trained Monsieur Ritz' chefs, the hotels grew famous—and the ex-waiter became dictator of the fashionable world.

Ritz Meringues

1 egg white	3 tablespoons granulated
½ teaspoon flavoring	sugar

Beat white until very stiff and dry. Add 2 tablespoons of sugar, little by little, and continue beating. Add flavoring, and another spoonful of sugar, and beat until the mixture will hold shape. Drop like birds' nests on buttered baking sheet, and bake in a slow oven until firm—20 to 30 minutes.

*   *   *

Now I am going to tell you of a Savory, very patrician in name, called *King Edward the Seventh.* Auxanges' mother, who had cooked in her day for an English lord, made it for me. Her master, who hobnobbed with royalty, told her the King himself concocted it, and mixed it over a chafing dish for his cronies at Balmoral.

When the King was a little boy, he was as dull as could be.

"Bertie displayed a deep-seated repugnance to every form of mental exertion," wrote Queen Victoria.

But when his little sisters learned cooking—as all the Good Queen's daughters did—Bertie (as the family called him) tagged along, and contrived dishes fit for a king.

King Edward VII Savory

2 egg yolks	12 tablespoons grated Par-
1 egg white	mesan cheese
½ cup light cream	Rounds of toast

The eggs—less one white—are beaten slightly with the cream, in a saucepan attractive enough to bring to the table. Add cheese, and stir constantly over a slow fire until thick and creamy.

Hot rounds of toast are passed, and when the savory arrives in the litttle copper pan in which it was cooked, each person pours a spoonful or two over his toast.

When he grew up, Bertie had the most charming manners and the worst morals in British society. As an elderly Prince Hal, he took to collecting fancy uniforms and recipes. And when, after sixty years, Victoria's all-but-perpetual Prince of Wales ascended the throne, his cronies scattered. And M'Lord went to the Indies—and taught Auxanges' mother to make the King's own savory. It is so good that you might want to buy a little copper saucepan, as I did, to make it in. Mine is three inches deep, and three and a half inches across the bottom—and exactly right for bringing to the table.

*　　*　　*

When I began writing this book, I decided to try out every recipe as I went along. Some of them were old-timers that I hadn't cooked since Rainbow days. So I had some parties, and ran the old specialties off, three and four at a time. Then, between cocktails and canapés—and newburgs and brownies—I put on weight, which I wanted to take off in a hurry.

Now if you wear a size 12, you can just skip this. But if you wear a 14, and all of a sudden it's getting tight—then, my dear, pull up a chair.

A *Nine-Day-Wonder Diet* was published in *Harper's Bazaar* (March 15, 1941) and a similar one in *Good Housekeeping* (August 1941). But before the magazine articles appeared, I had read in a syndicated newspaper column,* these astounding words:

Reducing can be done quickly by confining the daily menu to lean meat, eggs, grapefruit and black coffee. . . . A pound a day for 10 days or more can be dropped.

After a long winter of eating everything I want, I diligently take off a few pounds annually—planning to shed them just before I get out of my winter coat. So I wrote Dr. Cutter, and asked him if he meant *only* "meat, eggs, grapefruit and coffee"— How about a few tomatoes, I asked—or a little spinach, and some lettuce?

"Re. your inquiry," the Doc. replied, "permissible, if taken with moderation."

Harper's diet allowed fruits, non-starchy vegetables, and an occasional sandwich. *Good Housekeeping's* advised the girls to eat a full quota of both raw and cooked green and leafy vegetables. It listed 28 vegetables (I never heard of some of them), and 18 fruits—and recommended buttermilk.

The schedules looked complicated, so I decided to stick with the Doctor—for simplicity's sake, and because I am not good at memorizing.

For breakfast I had half a grapefruit (unsweetened, of course), and a cup of black coffee.

At noon, I had any kind of lean meat I wanted, and a vegetable that everybody knows isn't fattening

* *Written by Dr. Irving S. Cutter.*

(tomatoes, spinach, string beans, broccoli, asparagus, or summer squash). I gave up salt entirely, and never tasted bread. If I didn't feel like meat, I had a couple scrambled eggs, usually with tomatoes. I bought some non-fattening mayonnaise, to use on vegetables and eggs in place of butter. And it was really very good.

At dinner I had the same things—with a clear soup, if I wanted it—and usually grapefruit for dessert.

Occasionally I had a whiskey and soda. And when I wanted it *very* much, I had ice cream—but never any sauce.

Every day I had the milkman leave a pint of skim milk (*modified* he called it!). And when it was icy-cold, it was pleasant to drink.

In a week, I lost eight pounds. And meat was the magic that did it—nice, juicy steaks, tender lamb chops, and lovely hamburgers—thick slices of sirloin, and good pot roasts.

Meat supplies strength, steps up metabolism, and burns up fat. And it is the only diet I ever heard of that eliminates fatigue, and keeps a woman good-natured.

Men are not so enamored of bones as some women think they are. And the girl who's skinny as a cigaret is sometimes nasty as a mink. But a good diet is a handy thing to know about, and this one is worth plugging.

Chapter Fourteen

Love in Bloom.

Half of the fun in a woman's life is falling in love. The other half is being in love. And throughout this book there has been a sort of theme song that might be called *Let's Have Fun*.

As a looker-on, I have watched the marriage game from the side-lines, and studied it with envy and compassion. I have observed the little women at work, and noted their tactics. I have seen them playing Queen and Slave, loafing like a WPA gang, and grafting like gold diggers. And I think Shakespeare was right when he said, "Maids are

182

May when they are maids, but the sky changes when they are wives."

Every girl who ever got through kindergarten has a technique for managing men. And if she got married, it worked. But when they cross the finish line, the girls relax. They don't use the energy trying to make a success of marriage that they did in persuading the boys to propose.

Matrimony is a let-down. Wives get on cozy terms with security, and take love easy. Girls who over-worked the siren strain in courting days get married, and give it a nice long rest.

Courtship was more fun than marriage:

> *How sad and bad and mad it was . . .*
> *But then how it was sweet!*

Make marriage a primrose path, and husbands will stick with it. Be fun to live with—and they should wander!

Love is more than just one stage. Marriage, like the world's, a play, where men and women have their exits and their entrances. And one girl, in her time, plays many parts. A wife's got to be an angel and a siren, cook and housekeeper, and a good sport with a gift for laughter and a maternal streak a yard wide . . . press agent, playmate, mistress, and pal.

Disraeli adored his homely old Mary Ann, because she was a good listener, she could talk politics, and she made wonderful apple tarts. They would open champagne at midnight, and discuss affairs of state while eating pie and cheese. . . . The trouble is there are not enough girls like Mary Ann.

Love, to begin with, is usually an emotional accident. And to make it last, we've got to work at it. The test of a person's intelligence is adaptability. And a clever girl has a flock of strings to her bow, and a repertoire that would make her grandmother awfully dizzy.

*   *   *

Men are easily taken in by blondes, red-heads (dyed and natural), honeysuckle girls from Dixie, and women named Myrna with large ear rings—but it is usually their wives' fault.

> *One would be in less danger*
> *From the wiles of the stranger,*
> *If one's own kin and kith*
> *Were more fun to be with.**

*   *   *

American men like spoiling women, and American wives are the most spoiled in the world.

It isn't being managed that men resent—but the sledge hammer technique. They love being worked

* Ogden Nash.

—but some women don't bother to do it artistically.

The silliest thing a woman can do is try to make a husband over. It requires humor and philosophy for any two persons to live together—and enough sense to make the best of realities.

Whoever pays for the sirloin and the Scotch should get a break in the bosom of the family, and a build-up. Every wife should bolster her husband's morale, and do a little press-agenting on the side.

Wives complain that husbands take them for granted, never pay them compliments, or notice what they have on. . . . But heart-hunger is not an exclusively feminine commodity. Men crave appreciation too—especially when they get pushed around in the office. And it's been a long time since some women told their husbands how wonderful they are.

On a date, a girl listens while the man talks about himself. She flatters, and cajoles, and pretends she is interested in all the things that interest him. She humors him, and babies him . . . then he proposes —and *bingo!*

Most women feel that once they have charmed a man into marrying them, it's nice going. Which is a comforting idea, but it never works.

"Now," says the lady, "he's mine—he can't get away." . . . And that is where the lady's wrong.

There never was a man with soul so dead he didn't hate possessiveness. You can drive a horse to water, but you can't make him drink. And you can drive a man to marriage, but you can't make him love.

Keep a man comfortable and well fed, and act as if you loved him—and you don't have to be beautiful or brilliant. More than anything else, a man wants things made easy and pleasant for him—and one human being to appreciate him.

*   *   *

There is no quality so profitable to a girl as amiability. Wives who go around looking as if they led secret lives of joy and happiness are good publicity for their husbands, and grand ads for matrimony.

"*Tout comprendre, c'est tout pardonner,*" said Catherine of Russia, that paragon of tolerance. Which was a pretty big statement, but a lovely idea. With most wives, to know all is to forgive a *little*. . . . Yet women forgive more easily than men —forgive and never forget.

Women, on the whole, are more honest, though not so straightforward, as men. Women often fool men, who are easily and eagerly fooled. But women are seldom deceived by men, except by choice. They see through deceit . . . and see through each other (you can't fool a woman about another woman).

A new husband may be impressed when you tell him about how you didn't let the butcher overcharge you, and how you made the girl at the stocking counter come across. He may even think you are smart the first few times. But *first trick ain' no trick,* as Auxanges used to say. And, by and by, he knows you're tough. (A woman knows you're stingy the first time.)

The line that separates judicious economy from tight-fisted meanness separates charm from close-ness—and a generous attitude toward life is a charming and gallant thing.

The qualities that men desire most in wives are affection, amiability, appreciation, sympathy, health —and the attributes of a good sport. . . . These are not any arbitrary notions of my own—I've bored every man I know to death, asking questions and writing down the answers.

The thing men dislike most is nagging. They dis-like shrews—women who scold, scream, find fault, and talk too much. . . . *Softly, softly,* said Auxanges —*softly catch de monkey.*

There is a man I know whose wife is a shrill and strident shrew. Once, when the tumult and the shouting died, a friend asked him how he stood it.

"George," he said, "I never hear her. I stopped listening ten years ago."

* * *

Men's pet peeves, like straws, are slight and silly— but look what happened to the camel.

It infuriates husbands to be asked to exchange or credit anything (especially milk bottles). They wish you wouldn't plan so many bridge parties, or ask them to go to the movies so often. And when they come home, "after a hard day's work" as they call it, they would be grateful if you didn't talk so much about the house, the children, and the neighbors.

Differences of opinion are usually unimportant to begin with. And the best way to dispose of a meaningless quarrel is to wash it up quickly. *Peace at any price* is a good marital motto. And if the next quarrel is partly your fault, here is a comeback to bail you out prettily. Just smile like a nice girl—not as if it hurt, or you didn't mean it, and don't sigh when you say,

"I'm sorry, darling."

Marriage takes the courage of a hero and the self-abnegation of a saint . . . but if you want it, it's worth it—and you'd better put your heart in it.

CPSIA information can be obtained
at www.ICGtesting.com
Printed in the USA
BVHW052258090223
658264BV00001B/72